NEW ZEALAND
Barbecue
COOKBOOK

Published by Hyndman Publishing
325 Purchas Road
RD 2 Amberley 7482

ISBN:
9781877382468

TEXT:
© Simon & Alison Holst

HOME ECONOMISTS:
Simon & Alison Holst, Michelle Gill

DESIGN:
Dileva Design Ltd.

PHOTOGRAPHY:
Lindsay Keats (except page 87, Sal Criscillo)
© Hyndman Publishing except pages 26, 28, 33, 52 and 53 New Holland Publishers (NZ) Ltd, and pages 11, 24, 31 and 59 Lindsay Keats.

FOOD STYLING:
Simon Holst

All rights reserved. No part of this publication may be reproduced, stored in a retrieval system, or transmitted in any form, or by means electronic, photocopying, recording or otherwise without prior permission of the publisher in writing.

The recipes in this book have been carefully tested by the author. The publisher and the author have made every effort to ensure that the instructions are accurate and safe, but they cannot accept liability for any resulting injury or loss or damage to property, whether direct or consequential.

The first time you make a recipe, check it towards the end of the suggested time to see if it is cooking faster, or more slowly than expected.

Always follow the detailed instructions given by manufacturers of your appliances and equipment, rather than the more general instructions given in these recipes.

Safety First

A barbecue provides an opportunity to relax and have fun with your family or friends. Make sure that no accidents spoil the enjoyment of the occasion.

- Make sure that your barbecue is correctly assembled and that it stands on a stable, even surface. Always follow the manufacturer's instructions for lighting and use.
- Make sure that a small child cannot touch a very hot surface by mistake. Keep hot utensils out of reach, too.
- Never leave a lit barbecue unattended.
- Never use a barbecue in an enclosed space – always ensure there is plenty of ventilation.
- Gas cylinders should be stored in a cool, dry place, preferably outside.
- When swapping or removing the cylinder for refilling, ensure that any valves on both the full and empty cylinders are turned off. Make sure that all connections are tightened properly before use and check by brushing soapy water around the joints; bubbles will form if there is a leak.
- Check flexible hoses regularly. Replace if signs of cracking or other deterioration appear. After replacement make sure that the ends of the hose are well secured and leakproof.

Food Safety

A barbecue should be a relaxed occasion, but there's no excuse to forget about food hygiene. Remember the four Cs: **C**lean, **C**ook, **C**over and **C**hill.

Clean
- Thoroughly wash and dry your hands before you handle food and/or start cooking, and keep them as clean as possible throughout the process.
- Ensure that both your barbecue and preparation area as well as your utensils are clean.
- Thoroughly clean utensils and scrub boards between preparation of raw and cooked foods (especially meats). Use separate plates to hold raw and cooked foods.

Cook
- Defrost frozen foods completely before cooking.
- Keep raw and cooked meats separate during cooking.
- Cook minced meats and sausages thoroughly until meat is no longer pink. Cook poultry until juices run clear when pierced at the thickest part. Use a meat thermometer if available.

Cover
- Keep foods covered and preferably chilled before cooking.
- Cover leftover cooked foods as soon as possible.

Chill
- Keep all perishable foods in the fridge until required.
- Cover meats and poultry and store them in the bottom of the fridge so they can't drip on other foods.
- If marinating meats for more than a few minutes, cover and marinate them in the fridge.
- Cover cooked foods and allow them to cool before refrigerating, but never leave at room temperature for longer than 2 hours.

Introduction

Now's the time to dust off your barbecue and make the most of those wonderful, lazy, hazy summer evenings!

Whether you have a large barbecue in your back yard, and use it to entertain your friends, neighbours, and all their children, or whether you keep a small, portable barbecue in the car boot and set it up at your favourite beach or riverbank to cook a romantic evening meal for two, we are sure you will find this book very useful.

- Try our luscious new ways with lamb and chicken
- Experiment with barbecued shellfish, foil-wrapped fish, celebration salmon or fish tacos
- Enjoy Asian-style beef salad, barbecued steak and home-made hamburgers
- Watch the way that vegetable kebabs and barbecued new potatoes disappear
- Spoon sensational home-made sauces and relishes over sizzling sausages
- Serve some of our super salads beside your barbecued meat or fish
- Delight the kids with finger food like honey-soy nibbles and wing-a-dings

We have always loved cooking on the barbecue, and are delighted to have the chance to share with you, some of the all-time family favourites that have been our summer standbys over the years.

We feel that interesting salads and side dishes can "make the meal", so we have included some new twists on old favourites. Summer is the perfect time to enjoy garden-fresh fruit and vegetables – and these will make the meat go further, too.

And, last but not least, don't forget barbecue breads! You can make your reputation with bruschetta, garlic bread, griddle scones or naan – all cooked on the barbecue!

Have fun, and enjoy!

Simon Holst and Alison Holst

CONTENTS

Barbecue Basics	4
Bastes and Marinades	7
Starters	8
Sausages	14
Lamb	16
Beef	28
Pork	36
Chicken	44
Fish	56
Vegetarian	66
Salads	72
Breads	82
Barbecue Accessories	85
Index	87

Which Barbecue?

There is a wide variety of barbecues available. You should be able to cook delicious food on the simplest of these, but if you are likely to use your barbecue a great deal it makes sense to take note of the various features offered on different barbecues, and decide exactly what you need before you make your choice.

Gas or Charcoal?

Gas barbecues are incredibly convenient. All you need to do is turn on the gas, light it, then wait a few minutes for it to heat up, and away you go. Once they are running, heat control is usually very simple, too – it's just a matter of turning a knob.

Purists, however, will say that a gas barbecue just doesn't give the same flavour as a traditional charcoal-fired barbecue. While this is true to some extent (see below), a charcoal barbecue does require more patience and organisation.

- The fire in a charcoal-fired barbecue should be lit at least 30 minutes before you want to start cooking.
- Arrange the briquettes in a pyramid in the middle of the barbecue, open the air vents (if there are any), place 2–3 firelighters into the lower part of the pyramid and light.
- When the flames have died down and the coals are covered in a grey ash, then the barbecue is ready to use.
- Heat is adjusted by opening or closing air vents, raising or lowering the grill racks and/or moving or rearranging the embers.

Portable Barbecues

Compact, and with a lid held in place when not in use by the angled legs that fold up over it (sometimes forming a handle), this is a good choice if you want to use your barbecue at different places. It's easy to put in a car, and store in a small place. However, you'll need a table or bench on which to stand it when it is in use. Because they are fairly small, they are best used for cooking only a few items or when catering for just two or three people.

Gas Barbecues on Moveable Trolleys

A barbecue fitted with wheels can be used in the most suitable part of your yard, and afterwards be wheeled away for storage. Shelves under the barbecue unit and foldaway shelves at the side are also useful features as they provide storage for the gas cylinder as well as food and various utensils. You need little extra table and bench space when storage space is built into your barbecue.

Domed Lids and/or Hoods

The lids that come with some barbecues are designed to partly cover food cooked at high heat, as well as cover food that will benefit from a smoky flavour and cooked at lower heat. They are of great advantage if you want to cook when the weather is not particularly warm, or if you want to cook large, fairly thick food items. Lids can be set ajar, and need not cover the whole barbecue. If your barbecue does not come

with any kind of lid or hood, you can make a foil tent to achieve much the same result, although it is not as efficient. Flat lids are designed to protect unlit barbecues from bad weather. They must never be put on while the barbecue is hot.

Windbreaks

Wind can slow down cooking considerably (obviously this will affect the cooking times we've given in this book). Windbreaks that offer protection on three sides are a great help in open, windy places or when you are barbecuing in a yard with little shelter.

Solid Plates

A solid metal hotplate gives you the option of cooking on a griddle or over direct heat. It's great for cooking foods such as bacon (which would otherwise drip more than desired), eggs and fish (as you would in a hot pan), and you may even wish to cook pikelets and pancakes on it. While a hotplate increases the versatility of the barbecue, food cooked on it will not have a smoky flavour (unless you use it in conjunction with a hood or lid). Some barbecues come with just a plate – i.e. no grilling rack.

Warming Racks

An extra rack above the cooking rack, on the far side from the cook, makes a good place to warm bread rolls etc, or to keep cooked food warm while other food is being cooked.

Pull-out Trays and Fat Collectors

A solid tray (under the grill rack) that pulls out for easy removal of fatty drippings makes clean-ups easier. This tray can be lined with foil, then with fine river sand, gravel or purpose-bought products for even easier disposal of fat etc.

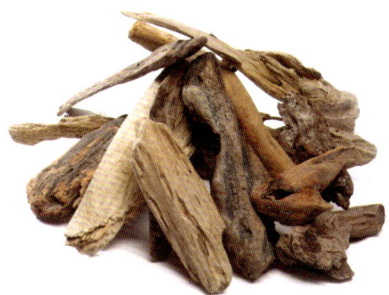

Gas vs Charcoal: That "Real" Barbecue Flavour

What makes barbecued food taste so good? When you grill food the conventional way, i.e. using your stove, its surface browns and cooks and some juices drip off the food to a cool area underneath the food, so your kitchen does not become smoky.

When you cook food on a rack above the hot coals of a charcoal-fired barbecue, the underside of the food cooks as the grilled food does, but the juices, instead of dripping onto a cool surface, fall onto the hot coals where they sizzle and smoke. This smoke gives the food its unique barbecued smoky flavour. When you cook the same food on a gas barbecue you can choose to plainly grill it or give it a smoky flavour. Placing a rack just above the gas flames and adding a layer of lava rock (scoria) or small ceramic bricks gives a similar effect to cooking over charcoal. The rocks or bricks are heated by the flames, then when juice from food drips onto them, they sizzle and smoke giving the food its "barbecue" flavour.

Using either a gas or charcoal barbecue, you can increase this smoky flavour by putting soaked hardwood chips on top of the hot rocks or embers (place them directly on top or use a holder). The wet chips smoke, rather than burn, and this extra smoke gives the food on the rack above a more marked flavour (fresh herbs or grapevine prunings can be used in the same way).

By covering the cooking food with a hood or domed lid (or a tent of heavy foil), you surround it with a warm atmosphere, and it cooks more quickly. This process also traps the smoke formed by the juices falling on the hot coals or from the smoking hardwood chips, thus intensifying the smoky flavour. Lava rock, pumice, and ceramic bricks may be re-used many times but soaked hardwood chips can only be used once.

Barbecuing Techniques

Barbecues can be used to cook in many different ways, however most people use them for cooking rather small items, for a fairly short time, generally on a grill or on a hotplate. Although you may start by barbecuing like this, you should be aware of all the other ways so you can make full use of your barbecue.

Cooking on a Grill

This method involves cooking over a grill or placing the food in a flat grilling basket over direct heat with the barbecue uncovered. The cooked food has browned outer surfaces, and a slightly smoky flavour. Pieces of meat big enough for individual servings, small whole fish, quickly cooked vegetables brushed with oil mixtures, and breads that are to be warmed through and lightly toasted are best cooked this way.

Cooking Large Pieces of Meat

Larger pieces of meat, which are to be cooked, then carved, call for different techniques. Use one of the following methods:

Turn the meat on a spit over the grill so that it cooks evenly on all sides and the centre heats through without the outside surfaces burning.

Cover the meat with the domed lid that comes with the barbecue (or less efficiently with a foil tent) so that the air around the meat heats via the embers or burners underneath and the meat roasts as well as browning.

Use indirect heat to cook the meat. This method is suitable for fairly large covered barbecues and involves covering the meat with a hood or domed lid so that the air around it is hot, but the meat is protected from the direct heat of the embers or element by placing it on a solid hotplate. (In the case of a two – or more – gas burner barbecue, position the meat over the unlit burner; the air under the lid will be heated by the other burner/s.) The indirect heat method can also be used on larger kettle-type barbecues where the briquettes or embers can be moved to the sides.

Smoking Food

Smoked food is produced by putting soaked hardwood chips on the hot rocks or embers. For maximum effect the food should be covered with a hood or domed lid so the smoke surrounds the food while it cooks. The soaked wood chips can be placed directly on the rocks/embers/burners or contained in a wide variety of purpose-designed holders.

Wrapping Food in Foil

Foil-wrapping enables many low-fat or very delicate foods to be heated on the barbecue in a steamy atmosphere without burning or falling to pieces before they have cooked. They will not have a browned surface or a barbecued flavour unless they are unwrapped and browned over the grill after they are tender.

Cooking on a Hotplate

Food cooked on a barbecue griddle or hotplate has little or no smoky flavour. Many foods that cannot be cooked directly on a grill can be cooked on a hotplate. In some cases though you can start a larger cut of meat on the grill to give it some smoky flavour, then transfer it to the hotplate to continue cooking without burning or excessive charring on the outside.

Cooking in Pots and Pans

Heavy pots, pans and kettles such as those made from cast iron can be used on a barbecue too. In this situation, as when using the hotplate, the barbecue is effectively an outdoor stovetop and as such the food will taste much the same as it would if cooked indoors. You can also heat up food cooked indoors in a heavy pot earlier in the day on the barbecue, ready to serve with your other barbecued foods.

Bastes and Marinades

Try some of these with different meats, fish and vegetables and feel free to experiment, changing proportions to suit your own preference.

LEMON BUTTER BASTE: Finely chop or crush 1 large garlic clove. Heat with 1 tablespoon butter until bubbling. Stir in 2 teaspoons light soy sauce or fish sauce and 1 tablespoon lemon juice. Brush on chicken or fish before and during cooking.

SESAME ONION MARINADE: Stir together 2 tablespoons Kikkoman soy sauce, 1 tablespoon onion juice (scraped from the cut surface of an onion cut through its equator), and 1–2 teaspoons sesame oil. Leave chicken, all meats and fish to stand in this before barbecuing, and brush on during cooking if desired.

MINTED YOGHURT SAUCE: Stir together ½ cup plain yoghurt, 1 tablespoon lemon juice, ½ teaspoon each of salt, ground cumin and sugar, 1 mashed and chopped garlic clove, and 2–3 tablespoons finely chopped mint. Leave to stand for at least half an hour, then marinate lamb in it, reserving the rest to use as a sauce over the barbecued lamb.

GARLIC HERB BUTTER: Chop together very finely in a food processor 3–4 peeled garlic cloves, 1 cup parsley sprigs, a few sprigs of thyme, dill, sage, or basil. Add 200g soft but not melted butter, a little lemon zest, and 1–2 tablespoons lemon juice. Season with black pepper and hot pepper sauce, process to mix, then refrigerate in a covered dish until required, up to 2 weeks. Melt small quantities to brush over fish, skinned chicken breasts or vegetable kebabs before barbecuing.

SOY AND SHERRY DIP: Simmer together until reduced to half original volume ¼ cup Kikkoman soy sauce, ¼ cup sherry, 2 tablespoons sugar, and 1 crushed garlic clove. Brush over any quick-cooking meat while it cooks, and drizzle some over the cooked meat.

LEMON AND GARLIC DIPPING SAUCE: Process together until finely chopped 2 tablespoons lemon juice, 2 cloves garlic, 1 small dried chilli, 2 tablespoons sugar, 2 tablespoons fish or light soy sauce, and 2 tablespoons hot water. Pour through a sieve, and add 1 finely chopped spring onion. Use as a dipping sauce or pour a few drops over barbecued fish, shellfish, lamb and vegetables. This is a wonderful sauce!

APRICOT MUSTARD GLAZE: Warm together 2 tablespoons apricot jam, 2 teaspoons mixed Dijon-type mustard, and 1 tablespoon dark or light soy sauce. Thin with a little sherry or orange juice if necessary until it is a good consistency to brush over nearly cooked lamb, chicken, or pork.

Additional Marinades

Tex-Mex Marinade	17	Festive Beef Marinade	35
Mediterranean Marinade	17	Honey-Soy Marinade	38
Sesame Marinade	17	Tandoori Marinade	50
East-West Marinade	17	Yoghurt Marinade	53
Wine Marinade	29	Grilled Fish Marinade	60
Asian-style Marinade	30		

Starters

Garlic Prawns

For 3 main or 6 starter servings:

500g frozen whole cooked prawns, thawed
3–4 cloves garlic, chopped
¼ cup dry white wine
¼ cup olive oil
¼ tsp salt
pepper to taste
2–3 Tbsp chopped parsley

There's something almost iconic about barbecued prawns, and these couldn't be easier.

Place the thawed prawns in a shallow dish. Add the remaining ingredients and stir gently to combine, then marinate in the fridge for 1–2 hours. Preheat the barbecue grill and cook the prawns briefly for 2–3 minutes per side.

Serve with crusty bread and a crisp green salad on the side.

Honey-soy Nibbles

2 Tbsp dark soy sauce
2 Tbsp honey
1 Tbsp Dijon or other mild mustard
1 clove garlic, crushed, peeled and chopped
1–2 tsp grated fresh ginger
1–2 tsp sesame oil (optional)
500–750g chicken nibbles or wings

Kids and adults alike love gnawing at these sweet and salty little morsels.

Measure the first five (or six if using the sesame oil) ingredients into a sturdy unpunctured plastic bag. Massage the bag to mix the marinade, then add the chicken pieces and massage again to coat. Gently squeeze as much air as you can out of the bag and leave to stand for at least 15 minutes (refrigerate if marinating for more than 20 minutes).

Cook on a well oiled (or baking paper or teflon lined) barbecue hotplate over a medium heat for 8–10 minutes per side or until the thickest pieces are cooked to the bone (the hotplate rather than the grill is best for these as the honey in the marinade can tend to blacken and burn over a naked flame).

Wing-a-dings

For 3–4 servings:

1 kg (about 10) chicken wings
1½ Tbsp Kikkoman soy sauce
1 Tbsp sesame oil or canola oil
2–3 cloves garlic, crushed

DIPPING SAUCE

3 Tbsp sugar
¼ cup boiling water
¼ cup fish sauce
1 Tbsp fresh lime juice
1 clove garlic, finely chopped
¼–½ tsp minced chilli
finely chopped coriander, carrot, cucumber and peanuts to garnish (optional)

Inexpensive chicken wings with a selection of dipping sauces make a good easy weekend snack and are always popular.

Put the chicken wings in a sturdy unpunctured plastic bag along with the next three ingredients. Knead the bag from the outside to coat the chicken evenly, squeeze as much air from the bag as you can and then leave at room temperature for 15 minutes or refrigerate up to 24 hours.

Preheat and oil the barbecue hotplate. Cook the wings over a medium heat for 8–10 minutes per side or until the thickest pieces are cooked to the bone.

Serve warm as finger food with a selection of dipping sauces such as sweet chilli sauce, hoisin sauce, oyster sauce or dipping sauce made by combining the ingredients in the order given. OR serve with a generous salad and crusty bread as a main meal.

Bacon-wrapped Savouries

Who can resist warm little savouries made by wrapping thinly cut bacon slices around fresh oysters or scallops, plump prunes, firm little button mushrooms or inviting chunks of pineapple? Barbecue them until the bacon is crispy and aromatic, and the filling is heated through but not overcooked.

Use thinly cut streaky but not too fatty bacon (available packaged at the supermarket). Cut the rind off each slice with a sharp knife or scissors, then stretch the bacon lengthwise. (Test wrap a savoury, allowing a little overlap, so you get the length of bacon required for each one just right.) If using wooden skewers to hold the bacon in place, presoak them to avoid burning during the cooking process.

Here are some ideas and preparation instructions for wrapping the following delicious treats in bacon:

Drain oysters and scallops on paper towels, and make sure that any grit is removed. Squeeze a little lime or lemon juice over them followed by a grind of pepper.

Pour boiling water over pitted prunes and leave to stand for 2–3 minutes, then drain and pat dry. Leave as they are or stuff with well drained water chestnuts, walnut halves, or pine nuts.

Cut the stems off button mushrooms, brush them with a damp paper towel or a soft brush. Sprinkle with a few drops of lemon juice and Worcestershire sauce, and your favourite infused olive oil. Wrap up a small sage leaf or a tiny sprig of fresh thyme with each mushroom if you like.

Cut fresh ripe pineapple into compact chunky wedges, removing the tougher core section. Sprinkle with a few drops of Angostura bitters and Tabasco sauce if you like.

Roll up the chosen items in the bacon, secure with the skewers and refrigerate until they are to be cooked.

Preheat and lightly oil the barbecue hotplate or grill. Arrange the savouries on the barbecue and cook for 6–10 minutes, turning as required, until the bacon is lightly browned and the fillings just heated through or cooked. Serve immediately, with plenty of small paper napkins.

Babaganoush

For about 1½ cups:
1 medium eggplant (300–400g)
1 medium-large clove garlic, peeled
2–3 Tbsp lemon juice
2 Tbsp tahini
3–4 Tbsp olive oil
about ½ tsp salt

We think eggplants are delicious, but we know there are those out there who are not so convinced. Even if you're not a great eggplant fan, you should try this tasty dip – it's really easy to make, and if you didn't know what was in it, we doubt you would ever guess.

Serve it with wedges of warmed pita bread or vegetable crudités or perhaps as part of a mezze platter with some marinated feta cheese and/or olives on the side.

Prick the eggplant in several places with a skewer, then microwave it whole on High (100%) power for 4–5 minutes, turning it after 2 minutes, until it is soft and wrinkly. Alternatively, bake it in a 180°C preheated oven for 35–45 minutes, or barbecue for 3–4 minutes on each of four sides until soft and wrinkly. Set aside until cool enough to handle.

Place the cooked eggplant on a chopping board, cut in half and scrape the flesh out of the skin. Place the flesh in a food processor fitted with the metal chopping blade, add the garlic, lemon juice and tahini, and process until smooth. With the motor running, drizzle in the olive oil and add the salt. Stop the processor, taste and add a little more salt if required.

Serve immediately or transfer to an airtight container and refrigerate for up to 1 week.

NOTE: tahini is a paste made from ground sesame seeds. Look for it in the refrigerated foods section of larger supermarkets; it's often in with the dips and dairy food.

Spicy Fish Cakes

For about 20 cakes:

3 slices white bread
½ medium red onion, peeled
300–400g fish fillets, roughly chopped
2 tsp red curry paste
1 Tbsp fish sauce
1 tsp sesame oil
½ tsp salt
½ tsp sugar
about ¼ cup chopped fresh coriander
1 medium carrot, grated
2–3 Tbsp olive or canola oil for frying
shredded lettuce to serve (optional)

DIPPING SAUCE

2 Tbsp lime or lemon juice
1 Tbsp each fish sauce and water
1 tsp sugar
finely chopped red chilli to taste
very finely chopped carrot and coriander to garnish

These make a great appetiser to pass around with drinks as a pre-dinner snack. Alternatively, if you come to like them as much as we do, they can be served with rice and a salad as a main meal. They are easy to cook on a lightly oiled barbecue hotplate – especially if you have a non-stick liner. Serve with the tangy dipping sauce in this recipe or a little Thai sweet chilli sauce.

Tear the bread slices into 4–6 pieces each and place in a food processor fitted with a metal chopping blade. Process until the bread is in crumbs no larger than peas. Chop the onion into 4–6 chunks and add to the crumbs along with the fish. Process until the fish is finely chopped, then add the next five ingredients and process until the mixture begins to form a ball. Add the coriander and carrot and process until just mixed.

Working with wet hands to prevent sticking, shape the mixture into walnut-sized balls, then flatten them into discs about 1.5cm thick.

Preheat the barbecue hotplate. While it heats, prepare the dipping sauce combining the first five ingredients in a small bowl. Stir until the sugar dissolves. Add the carrot and chopped coriander for colour.

Lightly oil the hotplate (or use a non-stick liner if you have one), then arrange as many of the cakes as will comfortably fit and cook over a medium heat until golden brown underneath, about 3 minutes. Gently turn the fishcakes one or two at a time and cook the other side.

Arrange on the shredded lettuce, if using, alongside a bowl of the dipping sauce and serve.

Flash-fried Paua

Although the inside of a paua shell is beautifully coloured, the tough, hard, muscular foot contained within looks very uninviting by comparison. If you are starting with paua in their shells, you should prise the flesh from the shell, discard everything except the muscular foot and the dark frilly part around it, and cut out the hard mouthpart from one edge.

Views vary concerning scrubbing and pounding the foot, but we have found that the end result can be excellent without doing either as long as the fleshy foot is cut into very thin slices (2–3mm) with a really sharp knife. (We have not cooked frozen sliced paua, but have been told that it is not particularly good.)

Preheat the barbecue hotplate. (Alternatively use a large, heavy frying pan over the grill.) When it is very hot, lightly oil it, or cover with a non-stick liner and add about 1 tablespoon of butter and some finely chopped garlic. As soon as the butter has melted, add the thinly sliced paua and stir-fry it. The paua will be at its most tender just after it has been heated through. Add a little lemon juice, some pepper and a dash of salt or light soy sauce.

Serve immediately, garnished with some finely chopped chives or spring onion, and with some crusty bread on the side.

Sausages

Super Snarlers

In all probability, if you grew up in New Zealand or Australia, a sausage was the first barbecued food you ever tasted. When treated with a little care, a barbecue can make a good job of cooking sausages. Nobody wants sausages charred on the outside and raw in the middle, yet many barbecued sausages finish up like this. There are several ways to avoid this problem.

Start with uncooked sausages of regular thickness, turn the heat to low, and move and rotate the sausages regularly, so that they heat through slowly and the centres cook before the outsides darken too much.

Choose long skinny sausages instead of thicker ones – they'll cook through faster, requiring half to three-quarters of the cooking time needed by regular sausages.

Buy precooked sausages, or precook your own sausages, before you take them outside to barbecue. When precooking, the important thing is to cook the centre of the sausages and reduce the amount of fat. Precook sausages just before you barbecue them or you can cook them in advance, then refrigerate them until required. To successfully precook sausages, gently simmer them with a little beer or water in a large covered saucepan until they feel firm, about 20 minutes. Discard the fatty cooking liquid. For larger numbers of sausages, bake in a covered roasting pan, with a little added liquid, for about 30 minutes at 150°C. To precook sausages in a microwave oven, place them in a single layer inside an oven bag or in a covered container, and allow about 15 minutes at Medium (50%) power for 500g of sausages.

Barbecue precooked sausages on a preheated hotplate or grill. Both give good results. For ease of turning a large number of small sausages, put them in a double-sided wire basket. Avoid barbecuing fatty, uncooked sausages as they tend to drip and produce a lot of fat.

Remember that all sausages were not created equal! There are many types of sausages available these days. Some are rather unmemorable but inexpensive, and need good sauces, relishes, breads and salads to turn them into an interesting meal, while at the other end of the sausage market are "designer sausages" that you can serve to anyone with pride.

Basic Sausages

Cheapest and most basic are packets of uncooked supermarket sausages. And because sausage meat is the cheapest meat of all, you can make your own sausages by combining the meat with chopped fresh herbs, grated cheese, Worcestershire sauce or whatever seasonings you like. Then, using wet hands, shape the mixture into patties. Do not coat the patties with crumbs if you are planning to cook them on the grill as they will burn easily (it's ok if you're going to cook them on the hotplate).

Flavoured Sausages

Many butchers, and some supermarket delis are selling interestingly flavoured sausages made from mixtures of pork, beef, lamb, venison, etc. These cost a little more, but are well worth trying on your barbecue at home.

Precooked Sausages

Precooked run of the mill sausages are now available from most butcheries. These are perfect for feeding large groups or if you're in a hurry, but are often fairly plain. If you are serving these make sure you include some interesting salads and/or sauces or salsas on the side. Alternatively, look out for cooked sausages in the style of frankfurters, which are often found in delicatessens. Usually more highly seasoned than the standard supermarket sausage, they may be heated by simmering in water or barbecuing. Try the plump red- and brown-skinned varieties as well as the thinner frankfurter size. Take care not to overcook them or they will shrivel and dry out. If you prefer, you can remove the casings before barbecuing.

Luncheon sausages and their more upmarket "cousins", including terrines, barbecue well too, when cut into thick slices or cubes and threaded on kebab skewers. Again, because they are already cooked, they require only to be lightly browned, and will dry out if overcooked.

Lamb

The flavour and texture of lamb make it very well suited to barbecuing. It can be cooked in many different forms: minced, cubed (loose or as kebabs), chops, and even larger cuts like whole boned legs or shoulders.

Barbecued Lamb Forequarter

If you like to carve and eat slices of lean lamb that are nicely browned and full of flavour on the outside, and pink, tender and succulent in the centre, try barbecuing a boned lamb forequarter. For maximum tenderness, prepare the meat and put it in its marinade in the refrigerator, one or even two days before you plan to cook it. Leftovers are good cold, so if you have a family of two or three you can enjoy the rest later.

Tex-Mex Marinade

1 Tbsp ground cumin
2 tsp oregano
½–1 tsp chilli powder
juice of 2 or 3 lemons
2 Tbsp Worcestershire sauce
2 Tbsp oil
2–3 cloves garlic, crushed

Mediterranean Marinade

Omit the chilli and replace the cumin with chopped fresh rosemary or thyme leaves.

Sesame Marinade

¼ cup Kikkoman soy sauce
¼ cup lemon juice
2 Tbsp sesame oil
1–2 tsp Tabasco sauce
2 garlic cloves, crushed

East-West Marinade

1 Tbsp dark or light soy sauce
1 Tbsp lemon juice
½ Tbsp honey
1–2 garlic cloves, crushed
1–2 tsp sesame oil (optional)

1 lamb or hogget forequarter, boned*

Tex-Mex, Mediterranean, Sesame or East-West Marinade

Remove any netting, string or skewers holding the boned meat together, and unroll the meat, skin-side down. Using a sharp knife, cut away any visible fat and membrane between the muscles, and snip any large chunky muscles so that the whole forequarter lies flat. Turn the meat over so that the skin side is up, and trim away as much fat as you can without the meat falling apart.

Put the trimmed meat in a sturdy unpunctured bag with the marinade ingredients of your choice (see opposite), and gently knead the bag to massage the marinade into the meat. Squeeze all the air from the bag, fasten with a rubber band, and refrigerate until about 4 hours before the meat is to be barbecued, then bring back to room temperature.

Place the meat, skin-side up, on the preheated, oiled grill of the barbecue. Cover with the hood or domed lid, or with a tent made from a doubled piece of foil (this traps heated air, so the upper surface of the meat is kept warm while the lower surface cooks). After about 10–15 minutes when all the lower surfaces are nicely browned, turn the lamb over and cook the other side. Under good conditions (refer page 4) the lamb will cook in 20–30 minutes and will feel springy, not spongy, when ready. If in doubt, cut open a thick part to see if the centre is done to the stage that you like. (Ideally insert a meat thermometer into the thickest part; it will read about 60–63°C when the lamb is cooked.) After the lamb is cooked, leave it to stand, covered, for at least 10 minutes, then carve in slices across the grain of the meat.

* These sometimes come rolled and tied or in a net.

Barbecued Leg of Lamb

A boned leg of lamb can be opened and trimmed to lie flat in the same way as a forequarter (see page 17). The meat is just as delicious, and as the leg is made up of several larger muscles than the forequarter the slices will be bigger.

However, boned rolled legs are not as freely available as boned forequarters. You can, however, ask any butcher to "butterfly" (i.e. open out) a boned leg or the shank end of a leg of lamb or hogget for you. If you explain that you want to barbecue it in one flattish piece, you may be able to get the outer fatty side trimmed too. Use the Tex-Mex or Mediterranean Marinade, and leave the boned leg to marinate for 24–48 hours before barbecuing. Cook as for a shoulder, increasing the cooking time to 30–40 minutes as the meat is thicker.

Lamb Racks

A lamb rack is cut from the front end of the loin. It consists of 6–8 rib chops in one piece, and is carefully trimmed. A chined, Frenched lamb rack with all its surface fat removed cooks on a barbecue in about 10 minutes and makes a gourmet meal for two. When a rack is chined by a butcher, all the bones except the curved pieces of rib bone are removed, so it is easy to carve between each chop. Because the sections of backbone are removed, the tender eye of rib meat cooks evenly. A rack is so tender that it does not need to be marinated, but it can be brushed with any of the lamb marinades in this chapter for extra flavour. Or try this one: heat a mixture of equal parts honey, lemon juice, and very finely chopped fresh mint, and brush over the lamb rack during the last few minutes of cooking. Spoon any remaining mixture over the carved chops. Barbecue on the grill over a high heat, bone side down, for about 5 minutes, then turn and cook on the other side for a further 5 minutes. Covering with the hood, a domed lid or foil tent as it cooks will speed up the process. The thick eye of meat should feel springy, not spongy, when cooked. Always leave a lamb rack to stand in a warm place for 5 minutes before carving between the bones.

NOTE: If the chops look too pink when the rack is carved, put the individual chops back on the barbecue for a brief period.

Lamb Chops and Cubes

For thousands of years the delicious smell of pieces of herb-flavoured lamb cooking over open fires has wafted through the southern European countryside.

You can quickly and easily barbecue chops cut from the shoulder, ribs, or middle loin. Like all meat which is to be barbecued, chops should be trimmed of as much visible fat as possible. Well-trimmed meat cooks much faster than meat surrounded by thick layers of fat, plus it does not drip fat and cause flare-ups.

Rib and middle loin chops are more tender than shoulder chops, and may be cooked without marinating if desired. Shoulder chops are best marinated for a few hours before cooking.

Rib Chops and Cutlets

Cut away nearly all outer fat. Cut off any knobbly bone with pruners or cutting pliers, if desired (in the case of cutlets, this bone will probably already have been removed).

Middle Loin Chops

Trim as much outer fat and other fat from the chops as possible without detaching the tail of the chop. To avoid overcooking tail meat, roll it up towards the small eye of very tender meat and secure with a toothpick.

Noisettes

Trim the fat as for middle loin chops as above, then cut around the T-shaped bone and remove it. Wind the tail around both eyes of meat, and push a wooden skewer through the rolled chop, from one side to the other. Cut off the skewer, and push the halved remaining skewer at right angles to the other so the crossed skewers will keep the roll of lamb flat and in place as it cooks.

Shoulder Chops

Cut off all outer fat and any bones which are near the edge of the chop. Snip the edges to prevent curling during cooking. Bang a few times on both sides with a meat hammer to tenderise if desired. Turn in desired marinade and leave to stand at room temperature for 1 hour or up to 24 hours in the refrigerator.

Seekh Kebabs

For 3–4 servings (8–12 kebabs):

½ medium onion
2 cloves garlic, peeled
2–3cm piece fresh ginger, peeled
500g minced lamb
1 tsp each ground cumin, coriander, garam masala and dried mint
1 tsp salt
½ tsp each chilli powder, ground cloves and cinnamon
8–12 wooden skewers soaked in cold water for 1 hour before using

Seekh Kebabs are made from seasoned minced lamb, shaped into "sausages" which are then skewered for support and cooked. You can make them smaller and serve them as an entrée, but they make a good main course when served on rice or with flat bread and a salad.

Place the onion, garlic and ginger in a food processor and process until very finely chopped (or mince very finely by hand).

Add the minced lamb and seasonings then process (or mix by hand) until combined. Knead in the processor, or by hand, until the mixture has a smooth even consistency (doing this will change the texture of the mince ensuring that it will not break up during cooking).

Divide the mixture into quarters, then each quarter into two or three smaller portions. With wet hands, shape each piece into a sausage shape 2–3cm thick and 10–12cm long. Spear each of these lengthwise with a skewer. Leave the kebabs in a round shape or flatten each one gently between your hands.

Preheat and lightly oil the barbecue grill. Cook the kebabs over a high heat for 4–5 minutes on each side or until nicely browned and no longer pink in the middle.

Serve as an entrée, or as the main part of a meal accompanied by rice and/or naan (or other flat bread) and a salad. Spoon herbed yoghurt sauce over them, if desired.

Herbed Yoghurt Sauce

1 cup plain unsweetened yoghurt
2–3 Tbsp finely chopped fresh mint
about ¼ cup chopped fresh coriander
1 Tbsp lemon or lime juice
½ tsp salt

Mix together all the ingredients and leave to stand for at least 15 minutes.

Lamb Kebabs

Cubes of lean lamb cut from any part of the carcase make good kebabs. Cheapest and most juicy are cubes cut from a boned forequarter or shoulder, or from shoulder chops. Although they may be cooked without marinating, they will become tenderised if left to stand in your favourite marinade for at least 1 hour before threading onto wooden or metal skewers. For extra colour and flavour, try alternating 2–3cm cubes of meat with similar-sized pieces of vegetable such as onion, zucchini, capsicums, mushrooms and cherry tomatoes.

Do not choose a marinade with a high sugar content: such a mixture is best brushed on during the last few minutes of cooking so it doesn't burn. If the meat is very lean, brush it with oil or an oil mixture before barbecuing. Cook on a preheated, lightly oiled grill over a high heat for about 5 minutes per side in good barbecue conditions. Cut into one of the cubes of meat to check whether it is cooked to the desired stage. Take particular care not to overcook kebabs which, if the cubes are small, may require less time.

Tapenade-rubbed Butterflied Lamb

For 6–8 servings:
1.2–1.5 kg butterflied shoulder or leg of lamb*
about ¼ cup tapenade (see the recipe below or use pre-prepared)
about 1 Tbsp olive oil

*If you can't find a butterflied leg/shoulder at your supermarket, ask them to prepare one for you – they'll usually do it while you wait.

A butterflied (boned, then spread out flat) shoulder or leg of lamb cooks really well, and surprisingly quickly, on the barbecue – and is great if you need something special. Tapenade is essentially a paste made from olives, anchovies and capers. It is sometimes served with bread or crostini as a dip or spread, but here we use it as a rub (rather like a very thick marinade) to flavour the lamb before barbecuing. We know olives and anchovies may not be everyone's favourite foods, but interestingly, despite their strong flavours, they don't dominate this dish, rather they just add a delicious savoury flavour.

Place the lamb on a board skin-side up and lightly score through the fat in a diamond pattern. Rub half the tapenade over that side of the meat, then turn it over and rub the remaining tapenade into the other side.

Place the meat in a large shallow dish, then cover with cling film and leave to stand for at least 15–20 minutes (refrigerate overnight if desired).

Preheat the barbecue (preferably hooded). Drizzle the lamb with the olive oil, then place it on the grill and cook, uncovered, over a high heat for 5 minutes per side, then transfer it to the hotplate and cook, covered if possible, over a medium-high heat for a further 10–12 minutes per side. (Ideally insert a meat thermometer into the thickest part; it will read about 60–63°C when the lamb is cooked.) Rest the lamb for 10 minutes before carving.

Serve with crusty bread and Greek Salad (page 73). Enjoy!

Tapenade

For about ½ cup:
1 clove garlic, peeled
125–150g pitted black olives
3–4 Tbsp lightly packed fresh parsley
3–4 anchovy fillets, plus oil in jar or container
1 Tbsp capers
1 Tbsp olive oil
1 Tbsp lemon juice
freshly ground black pepper

This makes more than you need for the recipe above, but the extra keeps in the fridge and can be used as a dip for vegetables or as a spread on bread or crostini.

Place the garlic, olives and parsley in a food processor and process until well chopped. Add the anchovy fillets plus 2–3 teaspoons of the oil they were packed in, and the capers. Process again until well mixed. Pour in the olive oil and lemon juice and process to make a smoothish paste (how smooth is up to you). Season with a little black pepper.

Use to coat the lamb as above or transfer to a clean airtight container and store in the fridge for 1–2 weeks. Serve with crackers or crostini and a selection of chopped fresh vegetables for dipping.

Fatoush with Lamb

For 4 servings:

2 small lamb rumps, about 500g in total
1 Tbsp lemon juice
1 Tbsp olive oil
1 tsp each cumin and paprika
4 medium pita breads
4 medium tomatoes
½ medium telegraph cucumber
1 green capsicum, cored, quartered and sliced
½ medium red onion, thinly sliced
½ cup mixture of chopped fresh coriander and mint leaves
½ tsp sugar
½–1 tsp salt
pepper to taste
3 Tbsp lemon juice
2 Tbsp olive oil

There's something about this delicious salad that just screams summer. The pita breads are an unusual and interesting addition – shortly after the salad is made they are slightly crunchy, but as the salad stands they soak up some of the juices and become almost meaty – either way they're good.

Place the lamb in a plastic bag with the lemon juice, the first measure of oil, cumin and paprika and leave to marinate for 15–20 minutes.

Preheat the barbecue and lightly oil the grill. Remove the lamb from the plastic bag and place on the heated grill. Cook for 3–4 minutes on each of the four sides with the hood of the barbecue down. You may want to cook them a little more or less, depending on the thickness of the meat and how well you like it cooked. Remove the lamb from the heat and leave to stand for 5–10 minutes before carving into slices about 5mm thick.

While the lamb cooks, place the pita bread on the grill for about 1 minute per side, then remove and set aside. When they are cool enough to handle, cut or tear them into bite-sized wedges.

Cut each tomato into 6–8 chunks and place in a large salad bowl. Halve the cucumber lengthwise and scoop out and discard the seeds. Cut the flesh into bite-sized chunks and add to the bowl along with the sliced capsicum, onion and chopped herbs.

Add the sliced lamb and pita bread wedges to the bowl and gently toss everything together. Sprinkle in the sugar and add salt and pepper to taste, drizzle with the lemon juice and second measure of olive oil, then toss again.

Taste and adjust seasonings if required before serving.

Jerk Lamb with Kiwifruit Salsa

For 3–4 servings:

½ small onion
2 cloves garlic
2 Tbsp olive or canola oil
1 Tbsp lime or lemon juice
1 tsp each paprika, cumin and dried thyme
½–1 tsp chilli powder
½ tsp each allspice, cinnamon and salt
about 750g lamb fillets*
1 Tbsp brown sugar

KIWIFRUIT SALSA

4 green kiwifruit, peeled and diced
2 cloves garlic, peeled and chopped
2 Tbsp Thai sweet chilli sauce
2 Tbsp lemon or lime juice
½ tsp salt
2–3 Tbsp chopped fresh coriander

Put the onion, garlic, oil and lime or lemon juice in a blender or food processor and process until smooth. Add the spices and salt and mix again.

Place the lamb in a plastic bag, then add the sugar and marinade mixture. Massage the bag to coat the meat, then seal the bag, squeezing out as much air as possible. Leave to stand for at least 1 hour.

Preheat and lightly oil the barbecue grill. While it heats, prepare the salsa. Place the prepared kiwifruit in a small bowl. Add the remaining ingredients and stir gently to combine. Leave to stand while the lamb cooks.

Gently shake any excess marinade off the lamb. Place the fillets on the grill and cook over a high heat for 3–4 minutes per side until browned and cooked as you want (slice through the thickest part of one fillet to check). Leave to stand for 3–4 minutes before slicing diagonally.

Serve the lamb drizzled with salsa and accompanied by plain or coconut rice.

* *Replace lamb fillets with shoulder chops, adding a mashed kiwifruit to the marinade mixture to tenderise the meat.*

Lamb Souvlaki

For 2–3 servings:
1 small-to-medium onion
3 cloves garlic
3 Tbsp olive oil
1 tsp cumin
1 tsp thyme
½ tsp oregano
½ tsp chilli powder
½–1 tsp ground black pepper
350–400g lean cubed lamb

TO SERVE:
½ cup natural yoghurt mixed with 2 Tbsp lemon or lime juice and ½ tsp paprika
about 2 cups shredded lettuce
about ¼ cup thinly sliced red onion
Tabouleh (page 77)
4–6 pita breads

Pita pockets stuffed with this tasty marinated lamb and salad make a great easy meal. Cook the lamb cubes "loose" or on skewers. Be warned – there is no tidy way to eat these. Fingers are best so provide plenty of napkins or paper towels.

Measure the first eight ingredients into a food processor or blender and process to form a smooth paste. Place the lamb in a bowl or plastic bag, then add the marinade paste and stir until the meat is well coated. Leave to stand for at least 20 minutes, but preferably longer. (For a really good flavour, the lamb can be marinated in the fridge overnight.)

If desired, thread the marinated lamb onto skewers or leave them "loose". Preheat and lightly oil the barbecue grill or hotplate (loose cubes are easier cooked on the hotplate). Cook over a medium–high heat, turning the skewers or pieces every 2–3 minutes or until the outside begins to blacken slightly but the inside remains a little pink. Allow the cooked meat to stand for about 5 minutes before serving.

While the lamb cooks, prepare the sauce by combining the yoghurt, lemon or lime juice and the paprika.

To serve, brush the pita breads with a little water or oil if they feel dry, and microwave them on High (100%) power for 15–20 seconds each. Halve and split the warmed pita breads, then fill each with a little shredded lettuce, some tabouleh, a few onion slices and 6–8 cubes of lamb. Add a spoonful or two of the yoghurt sauce and serve.

Lamb in Yoghurt and Honey

For 4 servings:
MARINADE
1 large clove garlic, peeled
2cm piece fresh ginger, peeled
½ cup plain unsweetened yoghurt
2 Tbsp lemon juice
1 Tbsp honey
2 good-sized sprigs of fresh mint or 1 tsp dried
1 tsp curry powder
½ tsp salt

500–600g lamb shoulder or loin chops

This simple but slightly different "from the norm" treatment of good old lamb chops can be served with rice and Raita for an Indian-style meal.

Place the marinade ingredients in a blender or food processor and process until smooth and evenly combined.

Arrange the chops in a shallow container in a single layer, then pour in the marinade. Turn the chops so they are coated with the marinade, then leave to stand at room temperature for 10–15 minutes.

Preheat and lightly oil the barbecue grill. Remove the chops from the marinade and arrange them on the grill. Cook over a medium heat for about 5–6 minutes per side.

Serve with rice and vegetables or a simple salad.

Beef

Barbecued Steak

Most of us eat steaks that have been cut 1–2cm thick and which are best cooked on a preheated thick metal hotplate rather than on a grill, since it is hard to get the grill hot enough to brown the outside of a thinnish steak without overcooking the centre. But if you have some steak around 3–5cm thick that you want to cook on the grill rather than on the hot plate, then carve it diagonally into thin slices before cooking. This method will give good results. All steaks will be more tender if they are marinated before they are cooked. The longer they stand in the marinade, the more tender they will be. Because marinades tenderise fastest at room temperature, if you have only a few hours in which to marinate steak, do it at room temperature. However, you can leave steak in a marinade in the refrigerator for several days, if you like. The tougher the steak cut, the longer it should be marinated. Put steak, trimmed of nearly all visible fat, in an unpunctured plastic bag with your chosen marinade, squeeze out all the air, and secure the bag with a rubber band.

- Fillet steak is the most tender steak.
- Rib eye and sirloin steaks are not quite as tender as fillet, but have more flavour.
- Rump steaks and cross-cut blade steaks have excellent flavour, but are tougher and require marinating and brief cooking for best results. A thick piece of marinated rump is excellent if carved after cooking.
- Thin flank or flank skirt steak may be marinated and cooked fairly rare, in one piece on a hotplate, then thinly sliced across the grain.

Wine Marinade

¼ cup red or white table wine
1 Tbsp wine vinegar
1–2 cloves garlic, crushed
1 tsp dried oregano
1–2 Tbsp corn or olive oil

Combine all the ingredients in a plastic bag as described above.

Any of the soy-based marinades used for lamb (page 17) are good for beef, too.

If your steak is not so tender, and you don't have much time for marinating it, tenderise it with a meat hammer before marinating it.

Pat the steak dry, oil its surface lightly, then brown on both sides on a thoroughly preheated hotplate (if you don't have a hotplate use a heavy frying pan on the grill). Lower heat and cook until the centre of the steak is cooked as you like it.

Cooking time can be as little as 3 minutes under good conditions (refer page 4). Brush with any desired glaze at end of cooking time.

Asian-style Beef Salad

Initially inspired by Thai beef salads, the ethnic boundaries of this dish have become a little blurred.

For 2–3 servings:

MARINADE

2 Tbsp each sweet chilli sauce and Kikkoman soy sauce

1 Tbsp each wine vinegar and sesame oil

300–450g thickly cut scotch fillet or rump steak

2 Tbsp lime or lemon juice

SALAD

¼–½ telegraph cucumber, halved lengthwise and sliced

1 red, orange or yellow capsicum, sliced

1–2 spring onions, thinly sliced

About 3 cups mesclun or mixed salad greens

¼ cup chopped fresh mint

¼ cup chopped fresh coriander

1 avocado, diced

Measure the ingredients for the marinade into a screw-top jar and shake to combine. Place the beef in an unpunctured plastic bag, then add half the marinade mixture. Massage the bag so the beef is covered with the marinade, then set aside for 30 minutes or longer (refrigerate overnight if desired). Add the lime or lemon juice to the remaining marinade, shake to combine then set aside.

Toss the prepared vegetables together with the spring onions, mesclun, mint, and coriander in a large bowl.

Preheat the barbecue to a high heat and lightly oil the hotplate. Remove the steaks from the marinade and place them on the hotplate. Cook for 2–3 minutes per side (you may need to vary the cooking time depending on the thickness of the steaks and how rare you want them). Remove the steaks from the hotplate and allow to rest for about 5 minutes before cutting into 5mm slices.

While the steak rests, peel and dice the avocado, then toss it with the other vegetables and half the remaining dressing. Arrange the salad greens on individual plates or on a platter. Fan the sliced meat over the greens, then drizzle with the remaining dressing.

Serve immediately, accompanied by some steamed fragrant rice if desired.

Barbecued Steak Sandwiches

This delicious American-style steak sandwich makes a substantial meal.

For 4 servings:

1 medium red onion (for marinade)

2 cloves garlic

¼ cup lemon juice

2 Tbsp soy sauce

2 tsp sesame oil

about 600g flank steak

1 Tbsp olive or canola oil

1 medium onion, peeled and sliced (for filling)

2–3 Tbsp mayonnaise

2–3 Tbsp Dijon mustard

1 French breadstick

lettuce or mesclun

sliced tomatoes

Peel and quarter the first onion. Place in a food processor or blender along with the next four ingredients and process until you have a smoothish paste.

Lay the steak on a board. Using a sharp knife, lightly score the surface in a diamond pattern. Repeat on the other side. Place the steak in a large plastic bag and pour in the onion marinade. Massage the bag so both sides of the steak are well covered with the paste, then squeeze out as much air as possible and leave to marinate for at least 15 minutes.

To cook, preheat the barbecue hotplate to a high heat. Remove the steak from the bag and gently shake off any excess marinade. Lightly non-stick spray the hotplate and place the steak on it. Cook for 3–4 minutes per side (flank steak needs to be rare or it will be tough), then remove from the heat and set aside to rest for about 5 minutes.

While the steak rests, heat the oil on the hotplate and cook the onion until soft and beginning to brown. Mix the mustard and mayonnaise together.

To serve, thinly slice the steak across the grain. Cut the breadstick into four pieces and slice each in half lengthwise. Spread each piece with the mustard-mayonnaise mixture. Divide the lettuce, sliced tomatoes, fried onion and sliced steak between the four pieces of bread, replace the tops and serve.

Thai-style Beef & Noodle Salad

For 2–3 servings:

about 300g flank steak
2 Tbsp each Kikkoman soy sauce and wine vinegar
1 Tbsp each brown sugar and sesame oil

DRESSING

3 Tbsp lime or lemon juice
1 Tbsp each fish sauce, brown sugar, peanut butter and grated fresh root ginger
1 large clove garlic, peeled and grated
chilli to taste

1 or 2 packets 2-minute noodles (oriental or chicken-flavoured)
½ small cabbage, shredded
2 tsp sesame oil
1–2 carrots, julienned or shredded
2 spring onions, sliced diagonally
6–8 cherry tomatoes, halved
2 Tbsp each chopped mint, coriander and roasted peanuts

This interesting salad makes a great meal for a warm night. It all needs to happen fast so you must prepare all the ingredients before you start cooking!

Put the steak in an unpunctured plastic bag with the next four ingredients. Set aside to stand for at least 5 minutes while you prepare everything else.

Put all the dressing ingredients in a small blender or hand-mix in a bowl. Mix well until creamy and smooth. Set aside until required.

Cook the noodles according to the packet instructions (use both packets for a more substantial meal, but discard the second flavour sachet), but do not drain. Stir the shredded cabbage into the undrained cooked noodles and leave for 2–3 minutes before draining. Return the noodles and cabbage back to the pot or large bowl and toss through the sesame oil. Add the carrots, onions and tomatoes, drizzle with the dressing, then toss together before arranging on a platter or serving plates.

Heat the barbecue grill or hotplate, then lightly rub with oil. Place the drained, marinated steak on the barbecue and cook for 2–2½ minutes per side until well browned but the inside is pink. Remove the steak from the barbecue and leave to rest for about 5 minutes.

Holding the knife diagonally, slice the cooked steak in strips about 5cm long across the grain of the meat. Place the sliced meat on the noodle salad, sprinkle with the mint, coriander and peanuts, and serve immediately.

Home-made Hamburgers

For 4 "quarter-pound" burgers:

500g minced beef
1 cup soft breadcrumbs (made from 2–3 slices bread)
1 large egg
1 tsp garlic salt
black pepper to taste

There's not much that beats a good home-made hamburger, and they're great cooked on the barbecue.

Place all the ingredients in a large bowl, then mix thoroughly (clean hands work best for this). Divide the mixture into four balls, then flatten each into a roundish pattie – it doesn't matter if they're not perfectly round. Refrigerate until required.

Preheat the barbecue and lightly oil the grill. Place the burgers on the grill and cook over a high heat for 2 minutes per side, then lower the heat to medium and cook for a further 2–3 minutes per side or until the centre is firm when pressed.

Serve in lightly toasted plain or sesame buns with three or four of the following:

- sliced tomato
- torn or shredded lettuce (or coleslaw)
- sliced cheese
- fried egg
- red, yellow and green capsicums (raw or roasted)
- sautéed mushrooms
- sliced gherkins or dill pickles
- thinly sliced red onion, crisped by soaking in cold water
- sliced avocado
- sliced beetroot
- watercress or other fresh herbs
- chilli beans and sour cream

Of course no burger is complete without tomato sauce and/or mustard.

Cajun Beef and Bean Burgers

For 4 large or 8 small burgers:

1 slice stale bread (or ½ cup soft breadcrumbs)
½ small onion, peeled
1 clove garlic, peeled
1 x 310g can kidney beans, drained and rinsed
400g lean minced beef
1 tsp cumin
1 tsp oregano
1 tsp salt
½ tsp chilli powder
½ tsp thyme
½ tsp ground black pepper

These burgers-with-a-twist have several nutritional advantages over conventional burgers – adding the beans effectively lowers the fat content and increases the fibre content at the same time. Most importantly perhaps, they also taste great!

Depending on whether or not you want to see the beans, you can make these burgers by either of two different methods.

Put the bread in a food processor fitted with the metal chopping blade and process into fine crumbs, then add the onion and garlic. Process again until finely chopped and well mixed. If you don't want the kidney beans to be seen, add them all at this stage and process until they are finely chopped. However, if you want them to show, add only half the beans at this stage. Add the mince and seasonings, then process until well mixed. If you reserved half the beans, add them now and stir them through the mince mixture or process again very briefly.

Working with clean wet hands, shape the mixture into four large or eight small patties. Cook and serve as per Home-made Hamburgers (above).

Sam's Beef Patties

The addition of black bean sauce to these patties gives them a hint of the exotic – it may see a little unlikely but it also seems to make them extra popular with children too.

For 12–18 patties:
3 slices (90–100g) bread
½ small-to-medium onion, peeled
500g beef mince
1 large egg
2–3 Tbsp black bean (or black bean and garlic) sauce

Tear the bread slices into quarters and place in a food processor fitted with the metal chopping blade. Process until finely crumbed, then transfer to a bowl. Add the onion to the processor and chop very finely. Tip the crumbs back into the processor, add the mince (broken into golf ball-sized pieces), the egg and the black bean sauce. Process in short bursts until evenly mixed (try not to over-mix or you will toughen the patties).

Divide the mixture into rough golf ball-sized portions and shape into patties about 2cm thick.

Preheat, then lightly oil the grill or hotplate and cook the patties over a medium-high heat for 3–5 minutes per side or until the largest patties are cooked through.

Festive Beef Fillet

For 6-8 servings:

1 kg beef fillet

MARINADE:

2 Tbsp wine vinegar or ¼ cup red or white table wine

2 Tbsp lemon or orange juice

2 cloves garlic, crushed

1 Tbsp light soy sauce

2 Tbsp olive or other oil

Although it may seem very extravagant to think about barbecuing beef fillets for a dozen or so people, this is not necessarily the case. From time to time small whole frozen beef fillets (weighing about 1 kilogram each) are sold by some large supermarkets for very reasonable prices. They can be kept in your freezer for up to 3 months. Slowly thawed and carefully cooked on a well-regulated barbecue, they may be served as the main part of a festive summer meal. They're just delicious – especially served with horseradish sauce or Dijon mustard, some simply cooked new potatoes and a salad or two.

Thaw small fillets slowly in the refrigerator. After 4–8 hours trim the meat, carefully cutting away the silvery membrane appearing on one side. This takes a little time but it is worth doing since it can shrink as it cooks, twisting the meat into a curved shape. Tie the trimmed fillet into a compact shape, tucking the narrow end under using a length of firm string or thread.

Place the prepared meat in the marinade, transfer to an unpunctured plastic bag and refrigerate for 1–2 days.

Take the meat from the refrigerator 1 hour before you are going to cook it.

Preheat the barbecue grill to a high heat and lightly oil. Place the fillet on the grill (along with a few sprigs of your favourite fresh herb to give a smoky, herby flavour). Cover with the hood or domed lid (or make a tent of doubled aluminium foil to enclose some hot air and speed up cooking.). Leave the heat high until the meat has browned on all sides.

Wait for about 7–8 minutes before turning the meat to allow it to heat through, then after 15 minutes or so reduce the heat to medium. The total cooking time for a 1 kg fillet is likely to be about 20 minutes. With experience, you can judge when the meat is cooked by pressing it – it should start to feel springy instead of spongy, or test it with a meat thermometer (63–65°C or 145–150°F for medium-rare or 70°C or 160°F for medium). Alternatively, make a cut in the thickest part and look at its colour or pierce it and look at the colour of the juices. They should be pink, but not bloody. Leave the meat to stand for 5–10 minutes before carving it into diagonal slices.

Delicious served with new potatoes and a salad.

Pork

Pork is another meat well suited to barbecuing. It is delicious in many different forms, from minced through to lovely lean pork loins, ham steaks or one of our all-time favourites, pork ribs.

Barbecued Pork Ribs

For 4 servings:
1½–2 kg meaty pork rib bones
1 cup water
sprinkling of ground cumin

1 onion
2 cloves garlic
1 Tbsp oil
1 tsp ground cumin
½ tsp ground coriander seed
½ cup tomato sauce
2 Tbsp Worcestershire sauce
2 Tbsp soft brown sugar
1 Tbsp wine or cider vinegar
1 Tbsp tomato concentrate
½ tsp cornflour
½ cup water
⅛–¼ tsp chilli powder

Although this recipe calls for preliminary work in the kitchen, it is worth it.

Cut the pork ribs into sections, each with three or four rib bones, and place in a large saucepan with the water and cumin. Cover tightly and simmer for 1½ hours or until the meat is very tender.

Barbecue Sauce

While the pork cooks, make the sauce. Put the first five sauce ingredients into a food processor and chop very finely. Transfer to a pan and cook over a moderate heat for about 5 minutes.

Measure the remaining ingredients into the pan, using chilli powder to taste, and simmer for about 15 minutes.

Place the precooked rib sections on a preheated and lightly oiled barbecue grill or hotplate and heat on each side until they sizzle. Brush with the warm sauce, and heat again on both sides.

Serve with crusty bread, warmed on the barbecue, or with corn cobs. Coleslaw goes well with either combination.

Stuffed Pork Fillet

For 3-4 servings:
2 pork fillets (200–250g each)
2 tsp mixed mustard
2 Tbsp light soy sauce
1 Tbsp olive oil
2–4 prunes
2–4 dried apricots
¼ cup orange juice
grated zest of ½ orange (optional)
1 Tbsp brandy (optional)
2 Tbsp pine nuts or chopped blanched almonds
1–2 tsp fresh rosemary and/or sage, finely chopped

This recipe is best suited to a barbecue with a hood or domed lid to keep the heat in and which will cook at a moderate rather than very high heat.

Lay the pork fillets on a board. Taking care not to cut all the way through, make a deep slit down the length of each fillet. Open out the fillets so they lie more or less flat and brush both sides with a mixture of mustard, soy sauce and oil. Leave to stand for about 15 minutes.

Open the prunes flat and quarter the dried apricots. Combine the orange juice and zest, if using, add the prunes and apricots and simmer in a saucepan over a low heat until the fruit is soft. Add the brandy and cook for a little longer until the liquid has almost disappeared, then arrange the mixture down the centre of one fillet. Top with pine nuts, and sprinkle with the chopped herbs. Cover with the remaining fillet so the wide end of one fillet is over the narrow end of the other. Skewer the fillets together with two rows of toothpicks. Brush with the remaining mustard, soy and oil mixture.

Cover with the hood, domed lid or a foil tent and barbecue for 20 minutes over a moderate heat, turning once after 10 minutes. If available, test with a meat thermometer (the pork is done when it reads 75°C or 165°F) or cut the fillets in half crosswise if necessary (when cooked, the fillet close to the fruit filling should just have lost its pinkness).

Leave to stand for 10 minutes before removing the toothpicks and carving. Serve with pasta, rice or crusty bread and a crisp green salad.

Glazed Pork Fillet

For 2 servings:
250g pork fillet, in one piece
1 small clove garlic, minced
½ tsp grated fresh ginger
½ tsp minced red chilli
2 tsp soy sauce
2 tsp sesame oil
1 Tbsp sherry
1 Tbsp apricot jam

Pork fillet is long and relatively thin – perfectly shaped for cooking on the barbecue. It is also very lean and should therefore not be overcooked to avoid it becoming dry.

Lay the fillet on a piece of sturdy plastic. Using the tip of a sharp knife, score both sides in a diamond pattern. Fold the plastic over the fillet and then bang both sides with a rolling pin until it is half the original thickness. Transfer the flattened meat to a plastic bag along with the next six ingredients. Knead the bag to mix and coat the meat, then leave to stand while the barbecue heats.

Preheat and lightly oil the barbecue grill to medium high or the hot plate to high. Take the fillet out of the bag, reserving the remaining marinade, and place it on the barbecue. Cook for 5–6 minutes per side. Towards the end of this time, press the fillet with your finger; it will firm up as it cooks.

Mix the remaining marinade with the apricot jam and brush over the fillet to glaze. Remove the fillet from the heat and leave it to stand for 1–2 minutes, then cut it in half diagonally. If it is still pink in the middle, microwave on High (100%) power for 1 minute, then leave to stand again.

Perfect served with a green salad and/or kumara salad.

Pork Kebabs

For 4 servings:
750g cubed pork
MARINADE
1 Tbsp dark soy sauce
1 rounded Tbsp honey
1 Tbsp sherry
1 Tbsp sesame oil
1 tsp grated fresh ginger
1 tsp Trappeys pepper sauce
2 cloves garlic, crushed
12 wooden skewers, soaked in cold water for 1 hour before using
OPTIONAL
3–4 pineapple rings
1 red capsicum
1 green capsicum

For these kebabs you can buy pork that's already cubed or choose foreloin, butterfly, or medallion pork steaks and cut them into cubes yourself.

Place the cubed pork in a sturdy unpunctured plastic bag. Measure the marinade ingredients into the bag, knead gently to mix, then squeeze all the air out of the bag, fasten with a rubber band and leave to stand at room temperature for at least 1 hour, or in the refrigerator overnight.

Thread the marinated pork onto the soaked skewers, alternating the cubes with chunks of pineapple and blanched red and green capsicum if desired. Barbecue on a preheated and lightly oiled grill or hotplate over a high heat. Turn the kebabs after 2 minutes, brushing with remaining marinade before and after turning. Test for doneness after 4 minutes (they are cooked as soon as pork feels firm and is no longer pink in the middle).

Tropical Pork Chops with Salsa

For 4 servings:
4 (2-3cm thick) pork chops
2 Tbsp lime juice
2 Tbsp dark rum
1 Tbsp brown sugar
2 cloves garlic, chopped
½ tsp cinnamon
½ tsp salt
1–2 Tbsp chopped coriander leaf

Hints of lime, rum, and cinnamon give these a delicious slightly exotic, tropical flavour. They're great served as is, but why not add to the tropical feel by trying them with the salsa below as well?

Arrange the chops in a shallow dish or sturdy plastic bag. Combine the marinade ingredients, then pour these over the chops. Turn the chops or massage the bag (squeeze as much air as you can out of the bag and fasten it with a rubber band or twist tie) so they are coated in the marinade. Leave to marinate for at least 20 minutes (or up to 24 hours in the fridge) turning once or twice. (This gives you a perfect opportunity to make the salsa!)

Preheat and lightly oil the barbecue grill. Place the chops on the grill and cook over a medium-high heat for 5-6 minutes per side. Leave to stand for a couple of minutes before serving with crusty bread, a salad and the salsa below.

Pineapple Salsa

¼ medium pineapple, peeled
½ red capsicum, deseeded
¼ red onion
2 Tbsp chopped coriander leaf
½-1 tsp minced red chilli
1 Tbsp lime juice
½ tsp salt

Cut the pineapple, red capsicum and red onion into 5mm cubes. Place in a medium-sized bowl. Add the remaining ingredients and stir to combine. Cover and refrigerate until required.

Japanese Pork Fillet

For 3–4 servings:
400–500g pork fillet
1 Tbsp grated fresh ginger
1 large clove garlic, finely chopped
2 Tbsp light soy sauce
pinch cayenne pepper
¼ cup sesame oil
3 Tbsp wine vinegar
1 tsp cornflour
2 Tbsp water

Don't be put off by the large amount of sesame oil in this delicious recipe. The flavour of the pork is wonderful when the exact amounts are used.

Trim the fillet of any fat and untidy ends if necessary. Put the fillet into an unpunctured plastic bag with the next six ingredients. Turn the bag to mix the ingredients and to coat the pork. Marinate for at least 30 minutes or for up to 24 hours (refrigerate the meat in the marinade over a longer time).

Preheat and lightly oil the barbecue grill or hotplate. Remove the fillet from the bag and reserve the marinade. Cook the pork for 4 minutes per side, then leave to stand for about 10 minutes before carving into 1cm slices. The meat should be cooked enough to lightly brown the outside and to cause the meat inside to turn from pink to light beige, with only a slight rosy glow in the centre. If you are not sure, cut the fillet in two crosswise. If there is still any bright pink flesh, cook for a little longer.

Mix the cornflour and water in a small saucepan or microwave jug. Add the reserved marinade and heat on High (100%) power until the mixture boils and thickens.

Serve the sliced pork drizzled with a little of the thickened sauce and a simple salad on the side.

Asian-style Pork Patties

For 4 servings:

1 cup breadcrumbs, made from 2–3 thick bread slices

250–300g pork mince

2 cloves garlic, crushed, peeled and chopped

1–2cm piece fresh ginger, finely grated

1 egg

½–1 tsp minced chilli (optional)

2 tsp sesame oil

1 Tbsp Kikkoman soy sauce

½ tsp salt

2–3 Tbsp chopped fresh coriander

If you make hamburgers regularly and want to make something a little different, try this delicious Asian-flavoured version. The shape doesn't really matter, but making them oblong or oval and serving them in long buns will emphasise they are something a little different.

Place all ingredients in a large bowl and mix thoroughly (clean hands work best for this). Divide the mixture into four balls, then flatten them into long oval patties – it doesn't matter if they're not perfect.

Barbecue on a preheated lightly oiled hotplate or grill, lightly browning both sides, then lower the heat and cook until the centres are firm.

Serve in lightly toasted hotdog buns or French bread with Oriental Coleslaw (page 77).

Barbecued Ham Steaks

For 4 servings:

4 ham steaks

GLAZE

¼ cup pineapple juice

1 Tbsp tomato or barbecue sauce

1 tsp mixed mustard (the smooth kind)

1 tsp cornflour

1 tsp light soy sauce

1 Tbsp maple syrup or brown sugar

Ham steaks are already cooked so need only be heated through and coated with a glaze to add a little sweetness. You can use pre-cut ham steaks for this recipe or cut thick slices from a boneless, pressed ham.

In a small saucepan mix together the glaze ingredients. Heat until boiling, stirring until the glaze is thick and clear. Snip the edges of each steak in 4–6 places so they will not curl up as they cook. Place the steaks in an unpunctured plastic bag or in a shallow dish and pour the glaze over them, ensuring they are coated on all sides. Leave for at least 15 minutes.

Barbecue over a high heat on a preheated hotplate or oiled grill for about 3–5 minutes per side until the steaks are hot and lightly browned on both sides. Do not overcook.

Barbecue a few canned pineapple rings to serve with each steak, if desired. This is best done on an oiled hotplate (alternatively, place the rings in a hinged wire basket to avoid breaking them when turned). If barbecuing fresh pineapple, lightly sprinkle slices or cubes with sugar before cooking.

Chicken barbecues beautifully. Although you can barbecue chicken in any form, it makes sense to concentrate on chicken which has been cut into smallish, flattish pieces, since these will cook more easily, evenly, and quickly than a whole chicken, chicken halves, or even a chicken that has been opened flat. You don't have to worry about tenderising the flesh, although you may want to marinate it for extra flavour.

Chicken

Barbecued Chicken Basics

Chicken Cooking Times

Cooking times vary so the suggested times that follow should be used as a guide only. Always make sure chicken is completely cooked by using a meat thermometer (it should read at least 80°C or 180°F) or by piercing a piece at the thickest part. As soon as the juice runs clear, not pink, the chicken is cooked.

Chicken Skin

Cooked chicken skin, although crunchy and delicious, is much fattier than the flesh underneath it. It can also drip fat onto embers or gas burners causing flare-ups that can result in burning or blackening the surface of the meat. You can avoid the problem by cooking skinless chicken pieces. Here are three ways of cooking skin-on chicken pieces with the minimum of problems:

- Precook chicken in a microwave oven, then brown it in a shorter time on the barbecue.
- Cook each piece over a fairly low heat, with the skin-side away from the heat, in which case it will need only a short time with the skin facing the heat.
- Turn the chicken pieces frequently so less fat drips from them.

Chicken Breasts

Chicken breasts are light and lean. Boneless, skinless chicken breasts may be barbecued whole, or cut in pieces and threaded on a skewer. They cook very quickly, may be marinated for flavour, and should always be brushed with oil or melted butter before they are cooked. They can be glazed towards the end of their cooking time for extra colour and for an attractive appearance. If you overcook them they will be dry, so watch them carefully.

Depending on the heat of the barbecue, a chicken breast can be cooked in as little as 4 minutes per side. (Test as described above.)

Chicken Legs

Whole (bone in) thighs and drumsticks are thicker than breast meat, and take longer to cook. It is easier to cook them without burning the outside if you skin them first or precook them in a microwave. Without precooking, they may take up to 30 minutes to barbecue. They are ready when the juices run clear, not pink. To precook chicken, microwave each thigh for 2 minutes and each drumstick for 1½ minutes on High (100%) full power.

Boneless Chicken Thighs

Choose boneless chicken thighs whenever possible. The flesh is moist and especially delicious. Opened flat, they cook very quickly, sometimes as fast as 3 minutes per side. Marinate them in a mixture containing some oil, and brush with extra marinade, or with a glaze as they cook.

Chicken Wings

Because they are so much smaller, chicken wing pieces cook faster than drumsticks. They have a high proportion of skin to flesh, and if not precooked may drip more than you want. Without precooking, they can take at least 20 minutes to cook.

Chicken Kebabs

You can buy ready-to-cook chicken kebabs at most supermarkets or make your own by skewering cubes of skinless chicken breast or boneless skinless chicken thigh meat, then marinating them in your favourite mixture before barbecuing them in a very short time.

To cook, preheat the barbecue grill to a high heat. Brush marinated kebabs with oil, melted butter or bacon fat. If you prefer your kebabs plain, i.e. unmarinated, brush them before cooking with a mixture of 1 tablespoon each of honey, lemon juice and oil, warmed together, or with Lemon Butter Baste (see page 7). When the grill is hot, oil or spray it with non-stick spray. Place the kebabs fairly close together on the hottest part of the grill, cook for 2 minutes, then turn and cook the other side for a further 2 minutes.

Kebabs are cooked as soon as they feel fairly firm when pressed. A further test is to cut a chicken cube in half to check that it is no longer translucent in the middle. Cook for a little longer if necessary, but take care not to overcook as the lean breast meat, which is very tender and moist if cooked to the right stage, dries out quickly.

"Shortcut" Barbecued Chicken Legs

Allow 1x 350g chicken legs per person

soy sauce

MUSTARDY CITRUS GLAZE

1 Tbsp wholegrain mustard

2 Tbsp lemon or lime juice

1 tsp grated lemon or lime zest

1 Tbsp olive or other oil

1 large clove garlic, peeled and finely grated

HOT SESAME GLAZE

2 Tbsp light soy sauce

2 Tbsp lemon juice

1 tsp brown sugar

2 tsp sesame oil

1 small fresh chilli, sliced, or 1 Tbsp Thai hot chilli sauce

SUNDRIED TOMATO GLAZE

1 Tbsp sundried tomato pesto

1 large clove garlic, peeled and finely grated

1 Tbsp balsamic or wine vinegar

½ tsp crumbled dried oregano

1 Tbsp olive oil

Precooking chicken legs before you take them outside to the barbecue really speeds up the process and removes doubt about doneness. Offer a choice of glazes, and you can serve the tasty, sizzling chicken only 10 minutes later.

Prepare the chicken legs well in advance. Brush the legs with enough soy sauce to coat them, then wrap in greaseproof or baking paper, or place in an oven bag. Microwave two legs at a time on Medium (70%) power for 7 minutes, turning once during cooking. The chicken is cooked when juice from the thickest part runs clear, not pink, when pierced.

If making more than one glaze, combine the relevant glaze ingredients in separate screw-top jars, shake well and refrigerate until needed. (Glazes will keep, refrigerated, for 1 week.)

Brush the precooked chicken legs with the glazes of choice and barbecue (or grill) for 8–10 minutes, turning to brown both sides. Brush with more glaze at intervals if desired.

Honey-lemon Grilled Chicken

For 4 servings:

2–3 cloves garlic, peeled

2 lemons

3 Tbsp manuka honey

2 Tbsp olive or avocado oil

1 Tbsp dark soy sauce

1 Tbsp chopped fresh thyme

4 large or 6–8 smaller (about 1 kg total) skinless, boneless chicken breasts

salt and pepper to taste

Honey adds a delicious sweetness to this tender chicken, while the lemon adds a little zing. It's great cooked on the barbecue or under the grill.

Place the garlic in a food processor and chop finely. Grate the zest from 1 lemon into the processor, then squeeze in the juice from both. Add the honey, oil, soy sauce and thyme, then process again until well mixed.

Place the chicken in a sturdy, unpunctured plastic bag. Pour in the marinade, then squeeze out as much air as possible before sealing the bag. Massage the sealed bag to coat the chicken evenly with the marinade and leave to stand for 20 minutes, or longer if you can (marinate and refrigerate overnight if desired).

To cook, preheat the barbecue grill, then brush lightly with oil. Remove the chicken from the marinade, season with salt and pepper, then cook over a medium heat for about 6–8 minutes per side, brushing once or twice with the remaining marinade. (If you are in doubt about whether it is cooked through, cut through the thickest piece at the thickest part to check there is no pink in the middle.)

Serve with a selection of salads alongside and some good bread.

Korean-style Barbecue Chicken

For 3-4 servings:

¼ cup Kikkoman soy sauce
1 Tbsp brown sugar
2 tsp sesame oil
1 Tbsp grated fresh ginger
2 cloves garlic, peeled and chopped
750g skinless, boneless chicken thighs*

TO SERVE:

lettuce leaves
grated carrot
steamed rice

*If you have the choice, smaller thighs are easier to serve.

These tasty chicken thighs can be cooked on the barbecue or under the grill.

Measure the soy sauce, brown sugar, sesame oil and ginger into a sturdy plastic bag or shallow dish that will just hold the chicken thighs when spread out in one layer. Add the chopped garlic, then massage the bag or stir the contents of the dish to combine.

Add the chicken, then massage the bag again to coat the chicken thighs in the marinade, then squeeze out as much air as possible and seal the bag. If using a dish, tip in the chicken, turn the thighs to coat in the marinade, then arrange them in a single layer before covering with cling film.

Leave to marinate at room temperature for 15 minutes (massage the bag or turn the chicken thighs in the dish once or twice during this period) or refrigerate for up to 24 hours, turning the chicken pieces occasionally. Remove them from the fridge and leave to stand at room temperature for 10–15 minutes before cooking.

Cook on a preheated, lightly oiled barbecue grill or place 5–10cm below a preheated grill for 5–6 minutes per side or until the thickest piece is cooked through (test by cutting through the thickest piece to check there is no pink in the middle). When cooked, transfer to a warmed serving dish.

To serve, pile a little grated carrot with some rice on a lettuce leaf, top with a piece of chicken, roll up loosely to enclose and eat.

Red-cooked Chicken

For 4 servings:

4 chicken legs (drum and thigh)
1 cup cold water
½ cup dark soy sauce
½ cup light soy sauce
2 Tbsp sherry
walnut-sized piece fresh ginger, peeled and sliced
1 clove garlic, peeled
1 star anise flower
1½ Tbsp sugar

Here is a recipe for barbecued chicken with a difference. The chicken is precooked in a strongly flavoured sauce before it is barbecued or grilled.

Combine all the marinade ingredients in an unpunctured oven bag, then add the chicken legs and massage to coat with the marinade. Microwave on High (100%) power for 12–14 minutes, or until the juices are no longer pink when one of the thighs is deeply pierced, turning pieces in the bag 2 or 3 times. Alternatively, simmer the chicken legs in the marinade in a covered saucepan for 15–30 minutes, turning once or twice. Test as above.

Pour off the cooking liquid, strain and refrigerate for reuse within a week or freeze it for later use.

Brown the chicken on the barbecue soon after precooking or refrigerate until required. Barbecue on a preheated and lightly oiled grill until lightly browned on both sides over a high heat if the chicken has just been precooked, or over a medium heat for a little longer if it has been refrigerated. (Remember it is already cooked and needs only reheating.)

Serve hot with barbecued fresh vegetables, warmed bread rolls and a leafy green salad.

Greek Barbecued Chicken

For 4 servings:

4 large or 8 small bone-in chicken pieces*
juice of 1 lemon
¼ cup olive or other oil
1 tsp paprika (optional)
2 cloves garlic, crushed
1 tsp oregano

* Choose chicken legs or quartered chickens for this recipe or thread wings or small pieces on skewers for easier turning during cooking. If necessary, break joints so pieces lie flat.

Cooked outdoors on a barbecue, or inside under a grill, this chicken is easy to prepare and cooks without fuss.

Put chicken with all the remaining ingredients in an unpunctured plastic bag. Leave to stand for 30 minutes, turning bag occasionally.

Preheat then lightly oil the barbecue grill, then arrange the chicken over a medium heat. Cook for 5 minutes per side over the grill, then transfer to the hotplate (if available) and cover with the hood, lid or a foil tent (page 4) and cook for a further 8–10 minutes per side. The chicken is cooked when the juices run clear, not pink, when the flesh closest to the bone at the thickest part is pierced (or a meat thermometer inserted at the same spot reads 80°C or 180°F).

Serve hot or at room temperature with a Mediterranean or a green salad.

Tandoori Chicken

For 4 servings:

3–4 cloves garlic
1–2cm fresh ginger
1 tsp each ground cumin, coriander, paprika, turmeric, dried mint and garam masala
½ tsp chilli powder
1 tsp salt
1 cup unsweetened yoghurt
8 small or 4 large chicken pieces, skin removed

This popular Indian dish is best prepared ahead and left in its marinade overnight (or at least for 1–2 hours). It cooks with little last-minute fuss.

Crush and chop the garlic and grate the ginger. Combine with the next 8 ingredients in a shallow container large enough to hold the chicken pieces in a single layer or in an unpunctured plastic bag. Stir in the yoghurt to make a paste. Add the chicken pieces, turning to make sure all are well coated with the spice paste.

Cover the container and leave to stand for 1–2 hours or refrigerate overnight if possible.

Preheat and lightly oil the barbecue grill, then arrange the chicken over a medium heat. Cook for 5 minutes per side, then transfer to the hotplate (if available) and cover with the hood, domed lid or a foil tent (page 4) and cook for a further 8–10 minutes per side. The chicken is cooked when the juices run clear, not pink, when the flesh closest to the bone at the thickest part is pierced (or a meat thermometer inserted at the same spot reads 80°C or 180°F).

Serve with plain rice, and/or naan bread (page 83) or salad.

Curried Chicken and Kumara Salad

Barbecuing is the perfect way to cook the chicken for this tasty salad as it really adds to the flavour.

For 2–3 large servings:

2 Tbsp natural unsweetened yoghurt
1 Tbsp sweet mango chutney
1 tsp curry powder
2 cloves garlic, minced
300–400g boneless, skinless chicken
500g kumara
2–3 sticks celery, sliced
½ cup roasted cashews or peanuts, roughly chopped
¼–½ cup chopped dates
¼ cup chopped fresh coriander

DRESSING

½ cup plain unsweetened yoghurt
1–2 Tbsp sweet mango chutney
1 tsp curry powder
1 tsp salt

Put the first measure of yoghurt, chutney and curry powder along with the chopped garlic into a plastic bag. Add the chicken, then massage the bag to coat evenly. Set aside for at least 15 minutes (refrigerate for longer periods).

Peel the kumara and cut into 2–3cm cubes. Cook until tender by either microwaving on High (100%) power in a covered container for 7–10 minutes or by boiling gently, draining, and leaving to cool to room temperature.

Preheat and lightly oil the barbecue and cook the chicken over a medium heat for 5–10 minutes on each side (depending on thickness) or until the outside has browned and the juices run clear when the chicken is pierced at the thickest part. Leave the chicken to stand for 5–10 minutes, then cut into bite-sized pieces.

While the chicken cooks, stir together the dressing ingredients and prepare the remaining salad ingredients.

Place the cooled kumara, chicken and salad (reserving a little of the coriander to garnish) in a large bowl, drizzle with the dressing, then toss gently to combine.

Garnish with the reserved coriander and serve immediately or refrigerate until required.

Yoghurt and Coriander Chicken Kebabs

For 2–3 servings:

MARINADE

2 large cloves garlic, crushed, peeled and chopped
2–3 Tbsp chopped fresh coriander
¼ cup plain unsweetened yoghurt
2 Tbsp lemon juice
1 tsp finely grated lemon zest
1 tsp paprika
1 tsp cumin
½ tsp salt
¼–½ tsp chilli powder (optional)
6–8 wooden skewers

KEBABS

400g boneless, skinless chicken breast, cut into 2–3cm cubes
1 medium red capsicum, deseeded and cut into 2cm squares
½ medium red onion, quartered and separated (optional)
2 medium zucchini, cut into 1cm slices

SAUCE

½ cup plain unsweetened yoghurt
2 Tbsp lemon juice
1–2 Tbsp chopped fresh coriander or mint
1 clove garlic, crushed, peeled and chopped
1 tsp paprika
salt to taste

This marinade gives these chicken kebabs an interesting Middle Eastern flavour – serve them with steamed rice and a salad or as a filling to be wrapped in pita or other flat breads.

Measure the marinade ingredients into a medium-sized bowl and stir to combine.

Stir the cubed chicken into the marinade, mix until well coated, then cover the bowl with cling film and leave to stand for at least 30 minutes. (Refrigerate if marinating for longer periods.) Soak the bamboo skewers in cold water while the chicken marinates to prevent them burning during cooking.

Thread the chicken and prepared vegetables onto the skewers, starting and finishing each kebab with a piece of chicken – this will help prevent anything falling off during cooking. Arrange the kebabs on a tray and brush with any remaining marinade.

Preheat the barbecue and lightly oil the grill. Prepare the sauce by combining all the ingredients in a small bowl.

When the barbecue is hot, place the kebabs on the oiled grill and cook over a medium-high heat for 5–7 minutes, then turn and cook for another 5–7 minutes. Check to see if the chicken is cooked through by cutting through a cube; it should no longer be pink in the middle. Remove the kebabs from the heat.

Serve the kebabs, drizzled with sauce, on steamed rice or tabouleh with a tomato or green salad, accompanied by warmed flat bread.

Chicken (Lamb or Beef) Satay

500g boneless, skinless chicken breasts (or lamb or beef schnitzels)
2 Tbsp soy sauce
2 Tbsp tomato sauce
1 clove garlic, crushed, peeled and chopped
1–2 tsp grated fresh ginger
10–15 wooden skewers

SATAY (PEANUT) SAUCE
1 Tbsp canola oil
1 small-to-medium onion, finely diced
1 clove garlic, crushed, peeled and chopped
1 cup hot water
½ cup crunchy peanut butter
2 Tbsp soy sauce
1 Tbsp brown sugar
juice of ½ lemon

If your kids like peanut butter, serve these tangy satay sticks with lashings of the easy peanut sauce. If they're not into nuts, the satay sticks are delicious as is or with good old tomato sauce.

Cut the chicken into 1.5–2cm cubes (or lamb or beef schnitzels into strips about 2cm wide) and place in a plastic bag or shallow bowl along with the soy and tomato sauces, garlic and ginger. Mix everything together and leave to marinate for at least 15 minutes (refrigerate if marinating for longer).

While the meat marinates make the sauce. Heat the oil in a medium-sized frypan, then add the onion and garlic and cook, stirring occasionally, until the onion is soft and clear. Add the remaining ingredients, stir well to combine and heat the sauce until it thickens and boils, then remove from the heat. Warm before serving if required.

Thread the marinated meat onto the soaked skewers (see page 85), then cook over a medium-high heat on a lightly oiled preheated grill or hotplate for 3–5 minutes per side or until cooked through (if in doubt, cut one of the thickest pieces of chicken in half to check it is cooked through).

Drizzle with the warm sauce and serve with plain rice and/or a salads.

Mexican Chicken

For 4 servings:
6–8 boneless, skinless chicken thighs or 4 chicken breasts
1 tsp each oil and butter
2 Tbsp Mexican Seasoning Mix or according to taste

This tasty and easy chicken uses a home-made seasoning mix.

Remove all skin and bone from the chicken meat.

Place the chicken between 2 pieces of cling film and bang with a rolling pin until they are approximately 1cm thick (snip thighs if necessary to make them lie flat). Brush with – or turn in – a mixture of melted butter and oil.

Sprinkle the chicken on both sides with some Mexican seasoning, using quantities to suit your taste (about 1 tsp per side gives a good flavour).

Preheat and lightly oil the barbecue grill. Cook the chicken over a high heat for 4–5 minutes per side (the chicken is cooked when you cut through the thickest part and the juices run clear rather than pink).

Serve with Barbecued Vegetables (page 79) or shred for use in tacos, burritos etc.

Mexican Seasoning Mix

1 Tbsp dried oregano
1 Tbsp paprika
1 Tbsp ground cumin
1 Tbsp garlic salt
1 Tbsp flour
2 tsp caster sugar
about 1 tsp chilli powder or to taste

This mixture is great used as a dry rub or as a marinade. Try it sprinkled over chicken breasts or thighs, on the steak of your choice, or even on barbecued vegetables.

Place the oregano in a mortar and pestle and grind it until it is in fine crumbs. Add it to a clean, dry screw-top jar with all the other ingredients. Screw on the lid, then shake to combine.

Fish

It's hard to beat a meal of freshly caught fish, lightly cooked to perfection on a barbecue! You can give your fish a smoky flavour, too, if you like (page 6).

Because fish is delicate, it must be handled carefully for good results. Double-sided hinged wire baskets, which are readily available, enable fish to be turned without it breaking up.

Whole Flounder or Sole

We think that barbecuing is the easiest and most delicious way to cook whole flatfish. Cut several parallel slashes on each side through to the bone, about 2–3cm apart. Brush both sides of the fish with Lemon Butter Baste (page 7), and place in a wire basket. Place the basket on the preheated grill over a high heat. Barbecue until the flesh flakes and looks milky when tested with a fork. This may be as soon as 2 minutes for a small whole fish, under good conditions (refer page 4). Turn the basket over to cook the fish on the other side. It is likely to take a slightly shorter time than the first side.

Barbecued Fish Steaks

Like flounder or sole, fish steaks are best cooked in a hinged wire basket on a preheated grill, or on the hotplate. Use Lemon Butter Baste or Garlic Herb Butter (page 7) to brush all surfaces before cooking. Cooking time will depend on the thickness of the steaks, but allow about 2 minutes per side for 2cm-thick steaks.

Barbecued Fish Fillets

Cook as above in a hinged wire basket on a preheated grill or hotplate. Take care that the thinner edges of fillets do not overcook before the centre is cooked. For this reason it is preferable to cook steaks rather than fillets because the former cook evenly.

Whole Round Fish

Fresh fish should be gutted (from as small a slit as possible) and the body cavity cleaned and filled with herbs, lemon slices, crushed garlic, sliced onion, etc. for extra flavour. It is not essential to scale the fish if you intend to peel back the skin before serving. If you wish to ensure even cooking, we recommend that you make several diagonal slashes in the thick flesh on each side of the fish. Brush both sides of the fish with melted butter or with Lemon Butter Baste (page 7). Another way to ensure even cooking is to make a layer of grape leaves between the coated fish flesh and the grill basket – definitely worth trying if you have grape leaves available. Cooking times vary enormously depending on the size and thickness of the fish, and cooking conditions, i.e. a thick fish will cook faster if a domed lid or foil tent is used to keep the top part warm while the bottom grills.

Barbecued Shellfish

We love to start a barbecue meal with mussels from the supermarket. We steam them open, taking great care not to overcook them as this will make any shellfish tough. When you cook mussels, make sure they are alive – their shells should be tightly closed or, if open, should close quickly when you tap them. Place them on the barbecue grill or in a hinged wire basket (the flat kind). As soon as the shells open slightly, lift them from the grill, drain off any liquid, and turn them the other way up. At this stage put a little Lemon and Garlic Dipping Sauce (page 7) or Garlic Herbed Butter (page 7) in each shell if you like. As soon as mussels are firm, but before they shrink and become tough, remove from heat. Serve on the half shell, on a flat platter, with whatever condiments you fancy.

Foil-wrapped Fish

1 whole fish, cleaned and gutted

SEASONING 1

1 tsp paprika

1 tsp garlic salt

1 tsp celery salt (optional)

1 tsp dill leaf

about ¼ tsp thyme

black pepper to taste

several sprigs of fresh herbs (e.g. dill, fennel, mint, cress, parsley etc.) (optional)

SEASONING 2

½ cup coconut cream

1–2 cloves garlic, peeled and chopped

1 Tbsp finely chopped fresh ginger

2 Tbsp soy sauce

½ tsp chilli powder

juice of 1 lemon

1 lemon (optional)

salt and pepper to taste

This no-fuss way of dealing with whole fish is handy because it is so versatile. You can use it with almost any type of fish (including trout) and you can vary the flavourings depending on what you have on hand – the only essentials are the fish and the foil – a lemon or two is a real bonus, but they can be omitted at a pinch. Here are two variations on the theme: one fairly traditional and the other with a more Pacific-Asian flavour. While both will work well with a cleaned fish of about 1 kg, exact quantities are not critical.

Make 2–3 deep slashes on both sides of the fish (this helps even cooking). Unless you want to eat the skin, the fish can be cooked unscaled as the skin will lift off easily once the fish is cooked. Make a double layer of foil large enough to securely wrap up the fish and place it on the bench (wider foil is a real help here).

Combine your choice of seasoning and sprinkle about a third of it over the foil where the fish will lie. Place the fish on top, rub or sprinkle a little of the seasoning mix into the cavity, then sprinkle the remainder over the top side. If you have a lemon handy, slice it thinly and slide a few slices underneath the fish, place a few on top, and stuff the rest into the cavity (you can add the optional fresh herbs in Version 1 at the same time).

Carefully fold up and seal the foil package, making sure there is no air around the fish. Place the package on the preheated barbecue or fire and cook, turning over every 5 minutes. As a very rough guide, allow about 10 minutes cooking per 500g fish, but the only accurate way to know if the fish is cooked is to open the package every now and then and check – when the flesh at the thickest part will flake, the fish is cooked. When the fish is cooked, remove it from the heat and leave to stand for about 10 minutes or until cool enough to handle.

Discard the head, tail and fins, then peel away the skin. Lift the flesh off the bones and place on clean foil or in a bowl and sprinkle with the cooking juices. Taste and season with salt and pepper if required.

Serve with rice, crusty bread or potatoes and a salad.

VARIATION: Use fish fillets (monkfish or snapper) and Seasoning 2 to make individual serving-sized packages. Allow 150–200g fish fillets per person and wrap either in smaller squares of foil or use squares of banana leaf (found in the frozen food section of Asian food stores) secured with a tooth pick. Cook as above, but reduce the time to about 4 minutes per side.

Fish Tacos

We had always thought that a taco was a folded, crisp fried tortilla. In the USA however, soft, filled tortillas like these were marketed as tacos. Whatever they are called, they are delicious and so easy to prepare!

For 2–3 servings:

300–400g fish fillets (e.g. tarakihi, gurnard or snapper)
juice of 1 lime (or 2 Tbsp lemon juice)
1 tsp ground cumin

SALSA

2 large ripe tomatoes
1 ripe avocado
¼ cup chopped coriander
1 spring onion, finely chopped
juice of 1 lime or 2 Tbsp lemon juice
½ tsp salt
½ tsp sugar

2–3 tsp olive or canola oil
6–10 soft corn tortillas
Tabasco or other chilli sauce to serve (optional)

Arrange the fish fillets in a shallow dish and sprinkle both sides with the lime juice, then sprinkle lightly with the cumin. Leave to stand while you prepare the salsa and any other accompaniments.

To make the salsa, halve the tomatoes then scoop out and discard the seeds. Cut the flesh into 7mm cubes and place in a bowl. Halve and peel the avocado. Cut into similar-sized cubes and add to the bowl. Add the remaining salsa ingredients and mix gently to combine.

Preheat the barbecue hotplate, then lightly oil it. Place the fish fillets on the hotplate and cook over a high heat for 2–3 minutes per side, depending on thickness, until just cooked through. Remove from the heat and place in a warmed serving dish. Alternatively, you can cook the fish fillets in a foil package (page 58).

While the fish cooks, warm the tortillas by placing them in a plastic bag and microwaving on High (100%) power for about 1 minute or warm each one briefly on the barbecue hotplate. In either case, wrap the tortillas in a clean dry tea towel to keep them warm.

To assemble, break the cooked fish into 4–5cm chunks and divide between the warmed tortillas. Add a generous spoonful of the salsa and roll up loosely. Serve with plain or green rice and a simple salad if desired.

NOTE: Soft corn tortillas are now available in long life packs in the Mexican foods section of larger supermarkets – keep a packet in the pantry so they're handy when the mood strikes.

Teriyaki-glazed Tuna on Brown Rice Salad

For 2 servings:

300–350g tuna loin steaks
2 Tbsp Kikkoman soy sauce
1 Tbsp each sherry and brown sugar
1 tsp grated fresh ginger
¼ tsp cornflour

SALAD

2 cups cooked brown rice
1 cup finely diced daikon
1 medium carrot, finely diced
½–1 cup finely diced cucumber
½ red capsicum, finely diced

DRESSING

1 Tbsp Kikkoman soy sauce
1 Tbsp sherry
1 Tbsp sesame oil
2 tsp white wine vinegar
1 tsp grated fresh ginger
1 tsp brown sugar
½ tsp salt

Tuna is delicious, and as far as fish goes it is sturdy enough to cope with barbecuing quite well. We like the tuna served with the salad below, but of course you can marinate and cook the tuna as described here, then serve it with the accompaniments of your choice.

Place the tuna in a sturdy unpunctured plastic bag and add the next four ingredients, reserving the cornflour for later use. Massage the bag to mix, then squeeze as much air as possible from it and leave to marinate, turning occasionally.

To make the salad, stir together the cooked rice and prepared vegetables. Whisk together the dressing ingredients in a small bowl, then stir the dressing through the rice mixture.

Preheat and lighty oil the barbecue grill. Lift the tuna from the marinade and place it on the hot grill. Cook for 2–3 minutes per side, depending how well you like your tuna cooked.

While the tuna cooks, transfer the remaining marinade to a small bowl and stir in the cornflour. Microwave on High (100%) power for about 1 minute or until thickened.

Spoon the salad onto plates, top with the cooked tuna, then drizzle with a little of the thickened marinade.

Marinated Grilled Fish

For 2 servings:

2 x 150–200g pieces boneless, skinless fish such as salmon or snapper, about 15mm thick

MARINADE

½ tsp ground cumin
¼ tsp dried oregano
¼ tsp chilli powder
½ tsp salt
1 Tbsp Dijon mustard
2 Tbsp lime or lemon juice
1 Tbsp chopped fresh coriander
1 clove garlic, finely chopped
2 tsp olive or other oil

Turn plain fish into a special occasion dish which will cook in 5 minutes!

Combine all the marinade ingredients in the order given in an unpunctured plastic bag big enough to hold the fish. Squeeze the bag to mix.

Place the fish in the bag and massage to coat. Leave to stand for 10–12 minutes.

Preheat the barbecue hot plate over a high heat. Fold over the edges of a doubled piece of foil, and coat its surface with butter or oil. Take the fish from its marinade and place on the prepared foil. Spread any remaining marinade over the fish.

About 6 minutes before you plan to eat, slip the fish, on the foil, onto the barbecue hotplate. Cover with the hood, domed lid or a double layered foil tent and cook over a high heat, until the fish flakes or has changed colour in the centre, usually after 5 minutes. The mixture on the outside of the fish is unlikely to change colour very much.

Nice with new potatoes and asparagus or salad vegetables.

Seared Scallop and Asparagus Salad

For 2-3 servings:

18–24 scallops
1 Tbsp sweet chilli sauce
1 Tbsp Kikkoman soy sauce
1 tsp sesame oil
50–75g rice noodles (vermicelli)
canola oil for frying
2–3 cups mixed salad vegetables (e.g. mesclun, sliced cucumber, capsicums, etc.)
1 bunch (200–250g) asparagus
1 Tbsp canola oil
about ¼ cup chopped fresh coriander

DRESSING

2 Tbsp each sweet chilli sauce, fish sauce and lemon juice
1 Tbsp oyster sauce
2 tsp sesame oil
1 Tbsp grated fresh ginger
1 clove garlic, minced
4 Tbsp water

This salad must be prepared in several stages, then assembled just before serving, but the results are definitely worth a little time and effort.

Mix the scallops with the first measure of sweet chilli sauce, soy sauce and sesame oil, then leave to stand while you prepare the remaining ingredients.

To make the dressing, measure all the ingredients into a medium-sized screw-top jar or blender and shake or blend until well combined.

Separate the rice vermicelli into two or three bundles. Heat 1–2cm of the canola oil in a pan or wok (the oil will be hot enough when a noodle that has been dropped in puffs up more or less instantly). Carefully drop in one bundle. When the first side has puffed up and turned slightly off-white turn it over using a fish slice or a pair of tongs, and cook until the other side has puffed up. Remove the cooked noodles from the pan and drain on paper towels. Repeat with the remaining bundle/s. (You can do this several hours in advance, then store the drained noodles in a sealed plastic bag.)

Place the prepared salad vegetables in a large bowl or plastic bag.

Preheat and lightly oil your barbecue grill and hotplate. Trim any tough ends from the asparagus, then place it in a plastic bag with the second measure of oil and toss it gently to coat. Remove the asparagus from the bag and place on the barbecue grill and cook for 3–4 minutes, turning occasionally until the spears are just tender. Remove from the barbecue and cut into 5–6 cm pieces. While the asparagus cooks, tip the scallops and marinade onto the hotplate (use a non-stick liner if available). Cook the scallops for 1–2 minutes, then carefully turn them and cook for a further 1–2 minutes or until just cooked.

Pour half the dressing over the salad vegetables and toss to combine. Arrange the salad on individual plates or a serving platter, then place the noodles over them. Pile the scallops and asparagus on top.

Drizzle over a little extra dressing and serve immediately. Don't worry if you have a little dressing left over; it keeps well in the fridge and can be used in other salads or even over warm or cold meats, chicken or fish.

See also

Bacon-wrapped Savouries	**10**
Flash Fried Paua	**13**
Garlic Prawns	**9**
Spicy Fish Cakes	**13**

Celebration Salmon

For 6–8 servings:

zest and juice of 1 orange and 1 lemon
¼ cup honey
1 Tbsp balsamic vinegar
1 Tbsp Kikkoman soy sauce
½ tsp salt
2 oranges, sliced
1 kg side of skin-on salmon, pin bones removed

We were bouncing round ideas for a slightly different idea for a festive Christmas dinner, and this is what we came up with! We wanted something with a unique New Zealand feel, reflecting our summer Christmas. What could be better than a delicious side of salmon cooked on the barbecue?

Make a glaze by heating in a non-stick frypan the citrus zest and juice, honey, vinegar, soy sauce and salt. Boil, stirring frequently, for 2–3 minutes. (Refrigerate in a covered container up to 3 days if desired.)

To barbecue, cook the glaze-coated salmon fillet in a double-sided hinged wire basket coated with non-stick spray, turning it once during cooking or without turning on the preheated, sprayed grill of a covered barbecue or on the preheated, foil-covered hotplate of a covered barbecue. (While the fish need not be turned, the top surface will not glaze as well. However, if a darker glaze is desired, brush the salmon with leftover glaze at least once while it cooks.)

Brown the glazed orange slices before or while the salmon cooks.

To check if the salmon is cooked, cut into the flesh at the thickest end (you can cover this cut with glazed orange slices before serving). When it has turned opaque right through, slide the cooked salmon onto a serving platter and arrange the glazed orange slices on top.

Serve hot, warm or cold, as is, or with any remaining glaze as a sauce, or with mayonnaise if cold.

Sweet Chilli Salmon on Sesame Noodles

For 2 servings:

about 300g salmon fillets, pin boned
¼ cup sweet chilli sauce
3–4 Tbsp chopped fresh coriander
1 Tbsp each lime or lemon juice and soy sauce
2 tsp sesame oil
½ tsp salt

200g noodles (e.g. Asian egg noodles, soba noodles, vermicelli, etc.)
1 medium carrot, julienned
10–15cm piece telegraph cucumber, julienned
about 100g daikon, julienned (optional)
1 Tbsp each canola oil, sesame oil and soy sauce
1 tsp grated fresh ginger
1 Tbsp toasted sesame seeds
salt and pepper to taste

We love this tasty salmon dish, and think it is particularly good served on a warm noodle salad, but you can, of course, serve it how you like.

Cut the salmon into serving-sized pieces, then place in a plastic bag and add the next six ingredients. Massage the bag to coat the salmon, then set aside.

Preheat the barbecue hotplate. Bring a large pot of lightly salted water to the boil. Add the noodles and cook until tender. While the noodles cook, prepare the vegetables. Drain the cooked noodles well and rinse briefly with cold water. Return the noodles to the cooking pot, add the remaining ingredients and toss to mix. Check seasoning and adjust to taste.

Arrange the marinated salmon pieces, skin-side down, on a double layer of foil and carefully place on the preheated hotplate. Cover the barbecue with the hood, domed lid or a double-layered foil tent and cook over a high heat for 5–6 minutes, depending on thickness.

Carefully slide the cooked salmon onto plates or a nest of the warm sesame-noodle mixture, drizzle with any remaining marinade from the foil, and serve immediately.

Salmon and Black Bean Parcels

For 4 servings:

2 Tbsp black bean sauce
2 Tbsp dry or medium sherry
2 tsp sesame oil
2–4 tsp grated fresh ginger
2 spring onions, thinly sliced
2–3 Tbsp chopped fresh coriander leaves
4 x 125g salmon steaks, each 2cm thick

These delicious salmon packages are flavoured with Oriental seasonings.

Combine the black bean sauce, sherry, sesame oil and grated ginger in a small bowl. In another bowl mix the spring onion and coriander.

Cut four sheets of foil each large enough to wrap, fold and seal a salmon steak. Working with one sheet at a time, place it on a dinner plate and sprinkle about an eighth of the coriander and onion mixture in the centre. Lay a salmon steak on top. Pour a quarter of the black bean mixture over the salmon, then sprinkle with another eighth of the coriander and onion mixture. Fold the foil over the fish to form a compact parcel, double folding then twisting or folding up the ends so no liquid will escape during cooking. Repeat with the remaining steaks.

Preheat the hotplate on a hooded barbecue, then arrange all four salmon parcels flat, with a little space between each, on the hotplate. Close the hood and cook the parcels for 6 minutes. Open one after this time and if the fish is just cooked through, it's ready.

Serve the sealed parcels promptly, on warmed plates with rice and green beans or bok choy, or a salad. Leftovers are delicious refrigerated and served cold.

Vegetarian

Vegetarian dishes may not be the first things that spring to mind when you think about barbecues, but there are some tasty ideas out there...

Brown Lentil Burgers

For 4–5 servings:

½ cup brown lentils
1 bay leaf
2 medium onions
2 cloves garlic
2 Tbsp oil or butter
1 Tbsp chopped fresh parsley
½ tsp dried basil
½ tsp dried marjoram
¼ tsp dried thyme
1 tsp salt
black pepper to taste
½ cup fresh wholemeal breadcrumbs
2 eggs
2 Tbsp tomato paste
2 tsp dark soy sauce
½ cup flour

These burgers take a little longer to make than conventional burgers, because the lentils have to be cooked first, but they have a good firm texture, much like that of conventional burgers, which makes them well suited to barbecuing.

Cover the lentils with water and boil with the bay leaf until they are tender, about 20 minutes. Remove from the heat, drain, discard the bay leaf, then transfer the cooked lentils to a large bowl.

Finely chop the onions and garlic and sauté in the oil until the onion is soft and clear. Add the herbs, and the salt and pepper. Add the cooked onion mixture to the lentils and mix in the remaining ingredients.

Divide the mixture into 8–10 even-sized portions. Using wet hands to prevent the mixture sticking, shape each portion into a 10–12cm pattie. If the mixture won't hold its shape, add a few more breadcrumbs or a little more flour.

Preheat and lightly oil the barbecue hotplate (use a non-stick liner if you have one). Place the patties on the hotplate and cook over a medium-high heat until lightly browned on each side and firm when pressed in the middle.

Serve with bread rolls and salad as you would conventional hamburgers.

Stuffed Mushrooms

For 3–4 large servings or 6-8 starters:

2 slices wholemeal bread
1 clove garlic, peeled
1 Tbsp olive oil
1 Tbsp pesto
1 Tbsp grated Parmesan cheese
2–3 Tbsp chopped and pitted black olives
½ tsp fresh thyme or ¼ tsp dried
¼–½ tsp salt
¼ cup pine nuts
8 large (10–12cm) flat or 12–16 smaller (6–8cm) mushrooms
black pepper to taste

These tasty stuffed mushrooms are really versatile in that larger mushrooms make the dish into a great vegetarian main while a good quantity of smaller ones can be served as a starter or finger food. Either way, the filling can be prepared ahead in minutes and the mushrooms baked when required.

Tear the bread into smaller pieces and crumb in a food processor. Add the garlic and process briefly. Add the next six filling ingredients and process until just mixed (the mixture should stay as crumbs, not turn to paste). Tip in the pine nuts and whiz again to mix evenly.

Remove and discard the mushroom stems. Spoon the filling into the mushroom caps, dividing it evenly between them. Avoid packing it down.

Preheat and lightly oil the barbecue hotplate. Arrange the mushrooms on the hotplate, then cover with the hood, domed lid, or a double layered foil tent and cook for 10–12 minutes, or until the filling begins to brown. Remove from the barbecue and leave to stand for about 5 minutes before serving.

Serve as a starter or accompany with a salad and bread as a main.

Eggplant and Feta Rolls

For 10–12 rolls (5–6 servings):

2 small–medium eggplants (about 400g total)

3–4 Tbsp olive oil (plain, basil- or garlic-infused)

1 medium red capsicum

1–2 Tbsp balsamic vinegar

100–150g feta cheese

about 2 Tbsp chopped basil (or 10–12 basil leaves)

salt and pepper to taste

These delicious rolls are so simple to make, the following is more like a set of assembly instructions rather than a proper recipe. The longer thinner eggplants (about 6cm thick) are best for making small starter-sized rolls, but if you can't get these ones use halved slices from a larger eggplant. Alternatively, larger eggplants can be cut more thickly and used to make larger rolls for a scrumptious vegetarian main course.

Cut the eggplant/s lengthwise into 7mm slices. Lightly brush both sides of each slice with some oil.

Preheat and lightly oil the barbecue grill. Place the eggplant slices on the grill and cook for about 3–4 minutes on each side. Set the cooked eggplant aside until cool enough to handle.

While the eggplant cools, prepare the remaining ingredients. If using a fresh capsicum, cut the flesh from the core in flattish slices (the same number as you have of eggplant slices), brush with any remaining oil and cook the same way as the eggplant. Cut the feta into the same number of slices.

To assemble the rolls, lay out the eggplant slices on a board and brush lightly with the vinegar. Lay a slice of capsicum and feta across one end, add some basil, sprinkle with salt and pepper, then roll up.

Arrange on a serving plate, drizzle with a little extra oil if desired, and serve.

NOTE: If you're short of time, use char-grilled bottled red capsicum rather than cooking it yourself.

Char-grilled Vegetable and Feta Salad

For 4–6 servings:

1 medium eggplant
2–3 zucchini, green or yellow
1–2 red or yellow capsicums
1–2 bunches asparagus (optional)
10–12 spring onions
2–3 large flat Portabello mushrooms
2 cloves garlic, crushed, peeled and chopped
2 Tbsp olive oil
2 Tbsp balsamic vinegar
pinch salt
black pepper to taste

DRESSING

2 Tbsp olive oil
1 Tbsp balsamic vinegar
1 tsp wholegrain mustard
¼–½ tsp salt

4–6 cups mesclun salad mix
100–150g feta cheese, crumbled

We sometimes get together with several other families for a "BYO" barbecue. Most of us produce fairly standard barbecue fare (sausages, steak etc), but one friend, Mike, has come up with a variety of vegetables which he char-grills, then uses to form the basis of this impressive looking and delicious salad.

Cut the eggplant into 1.5–2cm thick slices, then cut the zucchini lengthwise into 1cm thick slices. Core, deseed and quarter the capsicums. Trim any tough ends from the asparagus if using, and trim the root ends and floppy green tops from the spring onions. Remove any protruding stems from the mushrooms.

Place the prepared vegetables in a large unpunctured plastic bag. Add the garlic, oil, vinegar, salt and pepper to taste, then gently turn the vegetables in the mixture until they are evenly coated. Set aside to marinate while you preheat the barbecue.

Lightly oil the barbecue grill. Cook the slower-cooking vegetables first (i.e. the eggplant, zucchini and capsicum), turning once or twice until softened and lightly browned, about 10–15 minutes in total. Remove the vegetables as they are done and set aside to stand until just warm.

Meanwhile, measure the dressing ingredients into a small screw-top jar and shake to combine.

Cut the warm vegetables into bite-sized pieces and spread the mesclun over a large platter. Just before serving, scatter the cooked vegetables evenly over the mesclun and sprinkle with the crumbled feta. Drizzle with the dressing and serve with plenty of crusty bread.

Eggplant Kebabs

For 4 servings:

2 cloves garlic, finely chopped
¼ cup olive oil
2 Tbsp sesame oil
2 Tbsp wine vinegar
1 Tbsp light soy sauce
1 tsp honey
1 tsp grated fresh ginger
½ tsp salt
200g eggplant, cut into 2cm cubes

Eggplant marinated in this mixture makes a good accompaniment for food from any part of the world.

Combine the first eight ingredients in a jar, or mix and briefly chop in a food processor or blender. Transfer to a shallow bowl and marinate the cubed eggplant in the mixture for about 30 minutes.

Thread the eggplant cubes onto medium-length wooden skewers that have been soaked in cold water.

Preheat and lightly oil the barbecue grill. Place the kebabs on the grill and cook until the cut flesh is evenly golden, turning frequently, for about 10 minutes. Brush with remaining marinade during cooking.

Serve hot, or at room temperature, with crusty bread and a tomato salad on the side.

Fresh Corn Cakes

For 3–4 servings:

1 cup self-raising flour
2 large eggs
½ cup beer or soda water or milk
2 Tbsp Thai sweet chilli sauce
1 tsp each cumin and paprika
½ tsp salt
1½ –2 cups fresh corn kernels (from 2–3 cobs)
2 spring onions, thinly sliced
2–3 Tbsp chopped fresh coriander
1 medium red or green capsicum, cored and diced

SALSA

2 firm ripe tomatoes, deseeded
1 medium avocado, peeled
½ red onion, peeled
1–2 Tbsp chopped fresh coriander leaves
1 Tbsp each lemon or lime juice and sweet chilli sauce
salt and pepper

These delicious corn cakes work well on a barbecue hotplate (especially if you have a non-stick liner) and make an interesting vegetarian option or brunch dish. They're particularly good topped with the salsa below, or for something even easier accompany with sweet chilli sauce.

Make the salsa first. Cut the tomatoes, avocado and onion into corn kernel-sized pieces, then toss together with the chopped coriander, lemon juice and sweet chilli sauce. Season to taste with salt and pepper, then leave to stand while you cook the fritters.

To make the cakes, measure the flour into a medium-sized bowl. Add the eggs, beer, chilli sauce, spices and salt, then whisk together to make a smooth batter.

Remove the husk and silk from the corn cobs, then use a sharp knife to slice off the kernels. Separate, then measure the kernels and add to the batter along with the remaining three ingredients.

Preheat and lightly oil the barbecue hotplate. Cook batches of cakes for 3–5 minutes per side until lightly browned on both sides and firm when pressed in the centre.

Sit cooked cakes on several layers of paper towels and keep warm in the oven until all the mixture is cooked. Serve immediately topped with the prepared salsa or bowls of sweet chilli sauce for dipping.

Cheesy Polenta with Barbecued Vegetables

Cheesy polenta topped with colourful barbecued vegetables makes a delicious treat for vegetarians or meat-eaters.

For 2–3 servings:

1 Tbsp olive oil or butter
2 cloves garlic, peeled and chopped
¼–½ tsp minced red chilli (optional)
1 cup quick cooking or regular polenta
3 cups vegetable stock or 3 cups water and 3 tsp instant vegetable stock powder
3 Tbsp grated Parmesan cheese
salt and pepper to taste

Heat the oil, garlic and the chilli, if using, in a medium-sized non-stick pan until it bubbles, then add the polenta and 2 cups of the stock. Stir until smooth, then cover and simmer for about 5 minutes. Add more stock until the mixture resembles very sloppy mashed potato, then cover and cook for a further 5 minutes for quick-cooking polenta or 10 minutes for regular polenta. Add extra stock or water to reach a soft mashed potato consistency.

Beat in the Parmesan cheese and enough salt and pepper to bring out its mild, pleasant flavour.

Barbecued Vegetables

Use a variety of different vegetables (and quantities) to suit yourself, but our favourites are: different-coloured capsicums, eggplants, zucchini, mushrooms – and asparagus when it's in season. Red onions or spring onions are also good because they add extra flavour and colour.

Prepare the vegetables as follows: quarter the capsicums, removing seeds and pith, cut the stems of the mushrooms so they are level with their caps, cut the eggplant into 1cm-thick slices, and the zucchini into 1cm-thick diagonal slices, and quarter small red onions lengthwise.

Brush the vegetables on all sides with olive oil (flavour it with a crushed, sliced garlic clove if desired). Preheat and lightly oil the barbecue grill and cook the vegetables for 5–10 minutes, turning once or twice, until they begin to soften or are as done as you like them. Brush with more olive oil mixed with your favourite pesto or with salad dressing just before serving piled over the polenta.

VARIATION: Serve barbecued vegetables with rice, pasta, or a couscous-based mixture, if preferred.

Salads are excellent accompaniments to barbecued foods. They not only taste good, but provide contrasting colour and texture as well.

Salads can be made from vegetables or you may decide to make more substantial "combination salads", such as potato, rice, or pasta and vegetable salads. These are especially good when you are feeding hungry teenagers or when you want to keep it simple with just some barbecued food and a salad.

Salads

Make sure your salads are interesting, varied, and served in sufficient quantities. Bowls of plain lettuce or tomatoes become boring, night after summer night. On the other hand, salads don't need to be complicated.

Here are some simple suggestions for raw vegetable salads to serve with your barbecued food or choose from those elsewhere in this chapter.

- Sliced tomato, mild onion rings and cucumber, sprinkled with salt, sugar and wine vinegar.
- Cubed tomatoes sprinkled with sugar, salt, pepper and chopped fresh basil.
- Long thin shreds of carrot with a little sesame oil and orange juice, sprinkled with chopped sultanas and chopped roasted peanuts.
- Sliced avocado sprinkled with lemon juice, pepper, salt, and thinly sliced spring onion.
- Sliced oranges (pith removed) with a little oil, wine vinegar and salt, with thinly sliced red onion and chopped mint.
- Shredded cabbage with celery, grated carrot and your other favourite coleslaw additions, dressed with mayonnaise-flavoured tomato sauce and smoke-flavoured salt, is excellent with barbecued meat. For a change, use a mustard-flavoured oil and vinegar dressing on coleslaw instead of mayonnaise.

Caprese Salad

For 4–6 servings:
4–6 ripe tomatoes
125–250g mozzarella cheese*
salt and pepper to taste
2 Tbsp olive oil
chopped fresh basil to garnish

The roundish balls of fresh mozzarella, usually packed in brine, are best for this salad (and taste quite different to the packaged blocks).

This colourful salad is an Italian classic and is as good served as a starter as it is as part of a buffet, a barbecue, or as a vegetarian option.

Cut the tomatoes into 1cm thick slices and thinly slice the mozzarella. Arrange alternating and overlapping slices of tomato and cheese on a flat plate. Sprinkle with salt and pepper to taste, then drizzle the olive oil over the salad. Top with the chopped fresh basil just before serving.

Greek Salad

For 3–4 servings:
6–8 small vine-ripened tomatoes or 1 punnet cherry tomatoes
1 green capsicum
½ telegraph cucumber
100–150g feta cheese, cubed
about 20 kalamata olives (optional)
2 Tbsp olive oil
1 Tbsp lemon juice
1 Tbsp chopped fresh basil and/or oregano
pinch of sugar
salt and pepper to taste

This simple salad makes a perfect accompaniment for barbecued meats, especially lamb. It is a great mixture of colours and textures and, of course, tastes great.

Quarter or halve the tomatoes (depending on size) and place in a medium-sized bowl. Core and deseed the capsicum, then cut into 2cm chunks. Quarter the cucumber lengthwise, then cut crosswise into 2cm chunks. Add the capsicum, cucumber, feta and olives, if using, to the tomatoes in the bowl and stir gently.

Measure in the olive oil and lemon juice, then add the fresh herb/s of your choice. Sprinkle with a pinch of sugar, then stir gently to combine. Taste, then add salt and pepper as desired.

Served chilled or at room temperature, this salad makes the ideal accompaniment to a barbecue or simple fish dish.

Elizabeth's Favourite Salad

For 4 servings:
1 Tbsp lemon juice
1 tsp sugar
¼ tsp salt
1 large avocado
2–3 firm, red tomatoes
10cm length telegraph cucumber
about 2 cups chopped crisp-leaf lettuce
1–2 spring onions
1 Tbsp olive or canola oil
freshly ground pepper to taste

Alison's granddaughters, Elizabeth and Jennifer, will at the drop of a hat make (and eat!) this ever-popular salad.

A short time before serving, mix the lemon juice, sugar and salt in a fairly large salad bowl. Stone and peel the avocado, then cut into 1cm cubes and turn gently in the lemon juice mixture. Cut the tomatoes and unpeeled cucumber into cubes and add to the other prepared ingredients. Chop the lettuce and add with the chopped spring onions to the salad bowl. Sprinkle with oil and pepper, and toss gently to mix.

Wilted Cucumber Salad

For 4–6 servings:
1 telegraph cucumber
1 tsp salt in 1 cup water
2 spring onions, chopped
1 small clove garlic, finely chopped (optional)
2 Tbsp wine vinegar
pinch chilli powder
1 Tbsp each toasted sesame seeds and sugar

A good side dish to go with lamb grilled on the barbecue and served with a peanutty sauce.

Halve the cucumber lengthwise. Using a teaspoon, scoop out and discard the seeds. Cut the cucumber into thin slices and place in the salted water for at least 10 minutes.

When ready to serve, drain the cucumber slices and place in a serving dish with the spring onion, garlic if using, vinegar and chilli powder. Crush the toasted sesame seeds and sugar in a pestle and mortar (or blender), add to the salad and mix well.

Marinated Tomato Salad

For 4 servings:
5–6 tomatoes
1 tsp sugar
¼–½ tsp salt
black pepper to taste
few drops Tabasco sauce
2–3 tsp wine vinegar
1 Tbsp chopped fresh basil, coriander leaves or parsley
1–2 Tbsp olive or canola oil (optional)

It's hard to beat this salad made from ripe, red tomatoes – ideally from your own garden!

Slice, quarter or cube the tomatoes into a serving dish.

About 10–15 minutes before serving, sprinkle the remaining ingredients, in the order given, over the tomatoes. Toss lightly and leave to stand at room temperature.

American Potato Salad

This is a wonderful salad if you make it with good quality mayonnaise. Make it the same day and refrigerate it promptly.

Put the cubed potatoes in a plastic bag, then add the vinegar and the oil. Mix gently, without breaking up the potatoes. Mix together in a shallow bowl the next three ingredients, then add the potato mixture and the chopped egg and fold through. Cover and refrigerate until ready to serve.

Just before serving, sprinkle with a little extra parsley.

For 2–3 servings:

2 cups cooked and cubed new or waxy potatoes
1 Tbsp wine vinegar
1 Tbsp olive oil
1 spring onion, finely chopped
2 Tbsp chopped parsley
¼ cup home-made mayonnaise or Best Foods Mayonnaise
½–1 large hard-boiled egg, peeled and chopped
extra chopped parsley

Kumara Salad

Kumara make very satisfying salads. Pick and choose from the recommended additions and be aware that the dressing is good with and without the sour cream or yoghurt.

About 6 servings:
3 medium orange-fleshed kumara
¼ cup sultanas
1 firm banana, peeled and sliced
¼–½ cup shredded coconut (optional)
2 spring onions, finely chopped
roasted peanuts or cashews (optional)

DRESSING
¼ cup olive or canola oil
¼ cup white wine vinegar
1 tsp Dijon or mild mustard
1–2 tsp grated fresh ginger
½ tsp salt
2 tsp sugar
¼ cup lite sour cream or plain low-fat yoghurt (optional)

Combine the first six dressing ingredients in a screw-topped jar and shake to mix. Add sour cream or yoghurt for a creamy dressing.

Scrub the kumara and microwave on High (100%) power for 5–6 minutes or until tender. When cool enough to handle, peel and chop into bite-sized pieces.

Pour boiling water over the sultanas to plump them up, then drain well and mix them through the kumara. Add the sliced banana, coconut, if using, and spring onion.

Toss half the dressing through the salad, adding more when serving, if desired. Sprinkle with the chopped nuts if using.

Couscous Tabouleh

It's not strictly traditional, but you can use couscous to make a really quick version of tabouleh.

For 3–4 servings:
¾ cup couscous
½ tsp each salt and minced red chilli
1¼ cups boiling water
2 spring onions
2 cups cubed red tomatoes
¼ cup each chopped mint and parsley
2 Tbsp each olive oil and lemon juice

Measure the couscous, salt and chilli in a medium-sized bowl. Stir in the boiling water. Cover and leave to stand, without stirring, for 5-6 minutes.

Finely slice the spring onions, cut the tomatoes into 1cm cubes, and finely chop the mint and parsley. Stir the herbs, vegetables, oil and lemon juice through the soaked couscous. Serve immediately or refrigerate until required.

Oriental Coleslaw

This is a slight twist on a perennial favourite. It makes an interesting change from the traditional version, and, not surprisingly, goes well with Asian-inspired dishes.

For 3–4 servings:
DRESSING
2 Tbsp canola oil
1 Tbsp Kikkoman soy sauce
1 Tbsp sweet chilli sauce
1 Tbsp rice wine vinegar or wine vinegar
1 tsp sesame oil

SALAD
2 cups shredded cabbage
2–3 sticks celery, thinly sliced
1 medium carrot, grated
1–2 spring onions, thinly sliced
handful roughly chopped coriander and/or mint leaves (optional)
chopped peanuts (optional)

Measure all the ingredients for the dressing into a screw-top jar and shake to combine.

Put the vegetables in a large bowl and toss to combine, adding just enough dressing to moisten everything (extra dressing will keep well in the fridge).

Curried Rice & Pineapple Salad

1 cup jasmine or basmati rice*
3 Tbsp canola or vegetable oil
1 small onion, peeled and finely diced
½ tsp mild curry powder
1 medium carrot, peeled and grated
½ cup frozen peas
¼–½ cup currants or raisins (optional)
1 x 225g can crushed pineapple, juice drained and reserved
2 Tbsp soy sauce
½–1 tsp salt
1–2 Tbsp chopped fresh mint and/or parsley

This type of salad is something of a journey back to Simon's childhood. Old fashioned it may be, but he still likes it, and more to the point so do his kids.

Put the rice on to cook (see below). While the rice cooks, heat the oil in a medium-sized pan, then add the onion and cook, stirring frequently, until soft and clear. Stir in the curry powder and cook for about 1 minute further, then remove the pan from the heat.

As soon as the rice is cooked, stir in the grated carrot, peas and currants or raisins, if using. Add the pineapple, 2 tablespoons of the reserved pineapple juice and the soy sauce to the onion mixture. Pour into the rice and mix well. Taste and season with the salt and fresh herbs.

Serve warm or refrigerate until required.

The easiest way I know of cooking rice is to combine 1 cup of it with 2 cups boiling water in a large microwave bowl and cook on Medium (50%) power for 15 minutes.

Ham & Pasta Salad

For 4 large servings:
250g short pasta shapes (e.g. spirals, bows etc)
1–2 Tbsp canola oil
100–150g sliced ham, cut into narrow strips
2–3 sticks celery, sliced
2 medium tomatoes, sliced
½ small red onion, diced
1–2 Tbsp chopped fresh chives or parsley to garnish

DRESSING
½ cup mayonnaise*
finely grated zest of 1 lemon
¼ cup lemon juice
2 Tbsp olive or canola oil
1 Tbsp wholegrain mustard
½ tsp salt
black pepper to taste

use good quality American-style mayonnaise or make your own

Ham and pasta salads are hardly a new idea – but they are always popular! Take care not to overcook the pasta or it will result in a soggy, unpleasant salad.

Cook the pasta in plenty of lightly salted boiling water according to the instructions on the packet. Drain the cooked pasta, then return it to the cooking pot filled with cold water. Drain again and repeat until the pasta is cool. Add the first measure of oil and toss gently.

Prepare the dressing by whisking together the first six dressing ingredients in a large bowl, then adding black pepper to taste.

Transfer the cooled pasta, ham and prepared vegetables to a bowl and add the dressing. Stir gently to combine. Garnish with the chopped herbs and serve immediately or store in the fridge until required (the salad can be prepared several hours in advance if desired).

Barbecued Vegetables

Vegetables are easy to barbecue if you remember two things:

- Because they are naturally low in fat, vegetables need to be brushed with oil or butter mixtures before and during cooking.
- For speed, precook denser vegetables by microwaving or briefly boiling them before barbecuing them.

Barbecued Potatoes

Although you will find barbecue recipes that call for raw potatoes, they take a VERY long time to cook. If you start with cooked potatoes, all you have to do is brown and crisp the outside while they heat through.

Prepare potatoes by scrubbing, then simmering them until just tender. Alternatively, scrub and quarter lengthwise 8 fairly large potatoes. Place in an oven bag with 25g butter and 2 tablespoons of water. Fasten the bag with a rubber band, leaving a finger-sized opening. Microwave on High (100%) power for 12–20 minutes until barely tender, twice repositioning the potatoes in the bag during the cooking time. Leave the potatoes in the bag until you are ready to barbecue them. Cook on a preheated, oiled grill or hotplate (use a non-stick liner if you have one), and turn to brown all sides evenly, brushing with flavoured butter or oil only if they burn. Allow up to 15 minutes for them to brown, depending on conditions.

Barbecued New Potatoes

Microwave 750g small potatoes with 1 tablespoon of butter, 2 mint sprigs and 2 tablespoons of water in an oven bag (see previous recipe) for about 8 minutes. Thread them onto skewers alone or with other vegetables. Brush with melted butter or Garlic Herb Butter (page 7) before cooking on an oiled grill until nicely browned.

Barbecued Mushrooms

Mushrooms barbecue well without precooking. Brush with Garlic Herb Butter, mayonnaise, or any oil-based dressing you like, then thread on presoaked wooden skewers and cook on a preheated grill or hotplate. For interesting vegetable kebabs, thread mushrooms with quick-cooking vegetables such as cherry tomatoes, or with precooked new potatoes, kumara, or chunks of lightly precooked red, yellow and green capsicums, etc. Brush with Garlic Herb or plain butter before barbecuing.

Cooked Vegetable Kebabs

Vegetables cut into 2cm chunks and precooked by brief boiling or microwaving can be threaded on presoaked wooden or metal kebab skewers, brushed with butter, oil, or any flavoured butter, and browned lightly on a preheated barbecue grill. Make colourful combinations of carrot, cauliflower, green, red or yellow capsicums, parsnip, pumpkin, kumara, zucchini and other summer squash, small whole onions or larger quartered onions. Brush your favourite glaze over kebabs just before serving if desired.

Barbecued Tomatoes

Small cherry tomatoes and quartered firm tomatoes may be skewered and barbecued with other quick-cooking vegetables. Large "meaty" halved tomatoes cook quickly on a heated hotplate or grill. Watch them carefully, though, because they turn very soft if barbecued too long.

Barbecued Corn Cobs

Young corn cobs (you know they're really young and fresh when the grains still have some milky liquid inside that you can see when you pierce them with a fingernail) may be barbecued in their green husks. Prepare them for barbecuing by pulling back the husk to remove the silk, then brushing the grains with garlic or plain butter. Rewrap in the husk, then wrap in foil if desired. Barbecue, turning frequently until all sides are very hot and exposed husks char, for about 5–10 minutes. Try them served with basil mayonnaise (page 80).

Don't barbecue dry looking very mature corn. Middle-aged cobs may be de-husked, brushed with butter and sealed in foil packages, then turned frequently on a hot grill until the grains are cooked. If preferred, you can precook the cobs, then butter them before wrapping them in foil to reheat only on the barbecue.

Barbecued Eggplant (Aubergine)

Thick slices or cubes of eggplant threaded on a skewer may be brushed with any well-flavoured oil and vinegar dressing, and barbecued on a hot grill until tender and browned. Because they may take longer than expected and need frequent basting, it is best to cook them separately, rather than on kebabs with quicker-cooking vegetables. Well-cooked aubergine has an interesting, meaty texture.

Barbecued Vegetable Salad

SEASONED OIL
½ cup olive oil
2 cloves garlic, peeled
6 fresh basil leaves, chopped
2 Tbsp chopped fresh thyme
2 Tbsp chopped fresh rosemary

Choose a colourful mixture of seasonal vegetables such as red onions, eggplants, zucchini, red and yellow capsicums, etc.

Cut your vegetables of choice into chunky pieces (quarter onions so pieces are held together by the root). Brush liberally with Seasoned Oil (see below) and barbecue over a medium heat, turning frequently so vegetables cook before they burn.

Allow vegetables to brown, but not burn on their edges.

Remove skins from capsicums if desired. Serve roasted vegetables warm or at room temperature. If desired, drizzle them with a little extra plain or seasoned oil, and a squeeze of lemon juice or a few drops of balsamic vinegar.

Serve garnished with black olives and sprigs of fresh herbs, if desired.

Seasoned Oil

Combine the ingredients in a food processor fitted with the metal chopping blade. Process until finely chopped. Allow to stand for at least 10 minutes then strain, discarding flavourings.

Roasted Red Onion Salad

For 4 servings:
4 red onions, quartered and barbecued without removing their roots
1 Tbsp olive oil
2 tsp wine vinegar
1 tsp balsamic vinegar
1 tsp sugar
½ tsp finely chopped fresh sage or thyme (optional)

Red onions are milder than other onions, and make an interesting and different salad.

While the onions roast, mix the remaining ingredients in a screw-top jar to make a dressing.

While they are still hot, transfer the roasted onions to a serving dish, sprinkle with dressing and turn lightly to coat, without breaking up the onions.

Serve warm or at room temperature (but not chilled) with barbecued foods.

VARIATION: Brush with Seasoned Oil (see above) instead of olive oil.

Basil Mayonnaise

For about 1½ cups:
1 egg
½ tsp each salt and sugar
1 tsp Dijon or mild mustard
1 Tbsp wine vinegar
about 1 cup olive or canola oil
about 10–12 fresh basil leaves, roughly torn

While you can now buy good quality mayonnaise, it's comparatively expensive when you consider that it's so quick and easy to make in the food processor.

Measure the first five ingredients into a food processor or blender. With the motor running, add the oil in a thin stream until the mayonnaise is as thick and creamy as you like. Once the mayonnaise has thickened, add the torn basil leaves and process again until these are finely chopped and have turned the mayonnaise a pale green colour.

Use immediately or keep in a covered container in the refrigerator for up to 7 days.

Bread makes a good addition to any barbecue and can be much more than simply buttered slices of white bread wrapped around tomato sauce-covered sausages, although for many children, this is a barbecue favourite.

You can use your barbecue to warm a variety of breads, and bread rolls, as well as toasting plain or buttered bread surfaces to make them really appetising.

Bread

Pita bread, after being warmed or lightly toasted, may be cut in half, opened, and filled with skewered meat, barbecued vegetables or salads. If you have trouble opening the bread to make it into a pocket, use it whole and just fold it round the food.

What's more, if you find that your family tends to stay around the barbecue after the main course, you can make griddle scones (closely related to the traditional damper of the past) on the hotplate, or in a heavy covered frying pan on the grill. Or let your children use the hotplate to cook spirals of scone dough wound around a stick. All of these are delicious served hot, with butter and strawberry or raspberry jam, or golden syrup.

Naan Bread

To make 8 naan:
3 tsp Surebake yeast
¾ cup warm water plus 2 Tbsp extra
¼ cup plain unsweetened yoghurt
50g butter, melted
1 tsp sugar
1 tsp salt
3 cups high-grade flour
extra butter or oil
sesame, onion or cumin seeds (optional)

Naan is an Indian flat bread. It may seem like an unusual thing to find in a barbecue book, but because naan is traditionally cooked in a tandoor (a charcoal-fired oven) it actually works really well on a barbecue hot plate.

Bread machine instructions

Carefully measure all the ingredients into a 750g capacity bread machine in the order specified by the manufacturer. Set to the DOUGH cycle and START. When the dough is ready, tip out onto a lightly floured surface and follow the instructions for shaping and cooking given below.

Handmade bread instructions

Measure the first six ingredients into a large bowl and mix well. Cover and leave for 15 minutes or longer in a warm place.

Stir in the flour, adding a little extra warm water or flour if necessary to make a dough just firm enough to knead. Knead with the dough hook of an electric mixer or by hand on a lightly floured surface for 10 minutes, adding a little extra water if it is too firm and minimum extra flour if it is too soft to work with (keeping the dough as soft as you can will produce good results). After kneading, the dough should form a soft ball that will spring back when gently pressed.

In a clean dry bowl, turn the dough in 2 teaspoons of oil, cover with cling film and leave in a warm draught-free place for 30 minutes. Turn out and knead lightly for about 1 minute.

Shaping and cooking

Divide the dough first into quarters, then halve again to give eight balls. Cover and leave to stand for 5 minutes.

Roll out each ball into an oval shape about 18cm wide and 22–23cm long. Brush each side with the extra melted butter or oil. Sprinkle with sesame, onion or cumin seeds if desired.

Preheat the barbecue hotplate until good and hot. Brush or wipe it lightly with oil, then place one or two (depending on the size of the hotplate) naan at a time on the hot plate, and cook for about 2 minutes on each side until puffed and lightly browned.

Serve immediately.

Bruschetta

2–3 Tbsp olive oil
1–2 Tbsp garlic-infused oil (or use plain oil and add 1 finely chopped garlic clove)
8–12 slices good quality French bread or ciabatta
salt to taste

Char-grilling gives good bread an amazing flavour, but you do have to be careful not to overdo it – no one enjoys burnt bread!

To make the bruschetta, preheat and lightly oil the barbecue grill.

Combine the oils (or olive oil and chopped garlic), then lightly brush both sides of each slice of bread. Season lightly with salt if desired.

Grill over a medium-high heat (watch carefully to prevent burning – it's amazing how fast it happens!) until golden brown on both sides.

Garlic Bread

200g soft butter
2 cloves garlic, finely chopped
2 Tbsp Parmesan cheese
2 Tbsp finely chopped parsley

Garlic bread is always popular, and can be cooked very successfully on the barbecue.

To prepare the seasoned butter, place the softened but not melted butter in a medium-sized bowl. Add the remaining ingredients and stir until well combined.

Slice a loaf of crunchy French bread, cutting not quite down to the bottom crust. (Cut the loaf in half first for easier handling if desired.) Spread 1–2 teaspoons of the flavoured butter between each slice.

Wrap the loaf in foil and refrigerate until required. Preheat the barbecue hotplate to a medium-high heat. Place the loaf on the hotplate, cover with the hood if your barbecue has one (but it's not essential), and cook for 8–12 minutes turning every 2–3 minutes. Unwrap and serve immediately.

Griddle Scones

For a 20cm scone or loaf:
2 cups self-raising flour
¼ cup sugar
½ tsp salt
½ cup milk
¼ cup canola or other oil

Griddle scones or damper must be one of the classic camping foods, and work well on the barbecue. It's a handy thing to be able to make if you don't have access to fresh bread, or just as an interesting side or even dessert.

Measure all the ingredients into a large bowl and mix to make a soft dough. Flatten the dough into a disc about 2cm thick.

Preheat and lightly oil the barbecue hotplate (or use a frypan over the grill or a barbecue liner if you have one). Carefully lift the dough onto the barbecue and cook over a medium heat for 5–6 minutes per side until browned and hollow sounding when tapped in the middle.

Serve alongside cooked meats, or split and serve hot with butter and jam.

VARIATION: Wind the dough around sticks and cook, turning frequently, on a hot lightly oiled grill.

Barbecue Tools and Utensils

Once you have your barbecue, investing in some useful bits and pieces will make your cooking easier and more efficient. These items also make great gifts for keen barbecue cooks.

- Before buying long-handled tongs, forks, turning slices etc, you should check to see whether you really need utensils with longer handles than those you already have in your kitchen. Implements with handles that are too long can be hard to manage.

- Long matches or a long lighter can be helpful when lighting gas barbecues that do not have 'built-in' igniters.

- A medium-sized stiff-bristled or wire brush is essential for removing residues from the grill rack.

- A basting brush (the size of a small paint brush) is a useful barbecue accessory; in fact, it would pay to have several for those times when you plan to use a variety of glazes, marinades and sauces.

- Hinged, flat grilling baskets made of wire are very useful for cooking foods that need to be turned often, or which may stick, then break when turned over. They come in different shapes and sizes with some holding only one or two small items such as hamburgers while others will hold a whole fish.

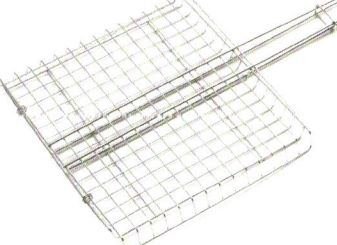

- If you plan to barbecue larger whole fish, you should get a proper fish-shaped wire basket.

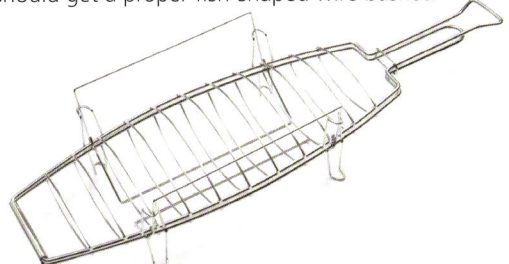

- A meat thermometer removes the guesswork when it comes to judging doneness (see the table on page 86). They are available in many forms: digital and conventional.

- A griddle or thick flat metal plate can be put on top of a grill if your barbecue does not come with its own hotplate. (Or use a heavy cast iron frying pan with a handle that will not burn in place of a griddle. A pan with a heavy, close-fitting lid can be used for cooking griddle scones, heating baked beans, etc.)

- Heavy-duty non-stick (Teflon) liners are available for use on barbecue hotplates. Because they can be used over and over again as well as making clean up easier, especially foods that are prone to sticking, they are a worthwhile investment.

- Skewers are very useful for keeping cubes and small foods in place. Metal skewers are, of course, reusable. When choosing metal skewers, look for those with flat sides that will stop food from slipping round.

- Bamboo or wooden skewers are inexpensive and disposable. If they are to be used for cooking that will take longer than a few minutes over direct heat, they should be soaked in water for at least 15 minutes before use. (Covering the ends with foil will also help prevent burning.)

- A roll of aluminium foil is a very useful barbecue accessory.

- Oven mitts and oven cloths will protect your hands.

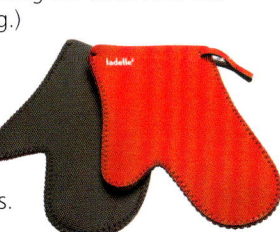

- Barbecue aprons can be entertaining as well as protective.

- Chopping and carving boards and knives are as important to have at hand as they are in the kitchen.

- A barbecue cover will protect the appliance from dust and grime if it is standing unused for some time.

Cleaning Your Barbecue

While you may feel that some modern appliances that have been designed to make cooking easier actually take longer to clean than to use, your barbecue definitely does NOT come into this category. In most cases the little cleaning that is necessary can be done outside.

Many of the spatters on the reusable lava rocks (or ceramic bricks) simply burn away. After use, they should be turned upside down so the side that has been dripped on now faces the burner/s. Turn on the gas for a while, and let those drippings burn to ash.

Barbecue grills

Burnt-on food residue can build up so it coats the grill. Some barbecues may have a grill (and hotplate) that has been treated with special coatings, in which case follow the manufacturer's instructions for cleaning. In other cases, we suggest you try our simple cleaning procedure.

When you have finished cooking, leave the barbecue going for 10–15 minutes, which will allow a lot of material to simply burn and turn to ash.

Scrape the grill with a metal scraper (there are many different types you can buy for this purpose).

Once the barbecue has cooled a bit, brush off the residue with a stiff bristle brush or better still a wire brush bought specially for the purpose. It is easier to do this regularly than to allow it to build up.

Finally, give the grill a light spray with oil or non-stick spray. If you don't have a spray can, a quick rub with some cooking oil-coated paper towels will do.

Barbecue hotplates

Wipe the hotplate with a wad of paper towels to remove excess fat or oil, then follow the cleaning instructions for the grill (see above), finishing with a light coat of oil or non-stick spray. Occasionally you may want to remove it altogether and give it a scrub using some detergent on a kitchen brush. Rinse with water, and replace ready for the next barbecue.

If your barbecue has a can or tray that holds the drippings from the food, empty it regularly. (A good tip is to line the drip tray with aluminium foil, then scatter river sand or gravel over it. When it needs replacing it's easy to wrap up the whole lot for disposal.) Don't let fat accumulate as if it overheats it can catch fire and burn.

Wipe the outer surfaces of the barbecue at intervals using a soft cloth or dish brush dipped in a mild detergent mixture. Make sure that layers of fat do not build up in hidden corners as they may flame up unexpectedly if they get hot enough.

Temperature Guide

Beef:	°C	°F
Rare	60	140
Medium-rare	63	145
Medium	71	160
Medium-well	75	165
Well Done (includes minced beef products such as hamburgers etc)	77	170
Lamb:		
Rare	60	140
Medium-rare	63	145
Medium	71	160
Well Done	77	170
Poultry:		
Chicken (breast)	79	175
Chicken/Turkey (whole)	82	180
(if stuffed, stuffing must reach 75°C/165°F)	75	165
Pork:		
Fresh Pork (Medium)	71	160
Fresh Pork (Well Done)	77	170
Ham (Fully Cooked)	60	140
Ham (Uncooked)	71	160

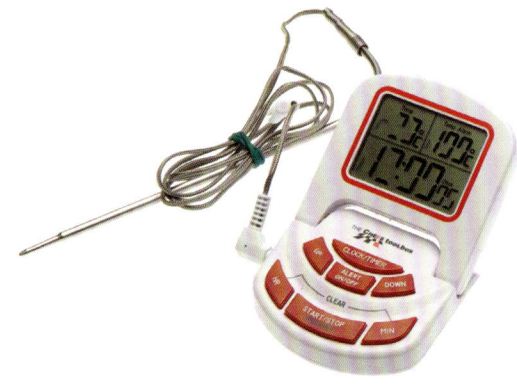

Index

American potato salad	76
Asian-style beef salad	30
Asian-style marinade	30
Asian-style pork patties	42
Asparagus and scallop salad	62
Avocado salsa	59
Babaganoush	11
Bacon-wrapped savouries	10
Barbecue chicken, Korean-style	49
Barbecue cleaning	86
Barbecue sauce	37
Barbecue utensils	85
Barbecued chicken basics	45
Barbecued chicken, Greek	50
Barbecued ham steaks	42
Barbecued lamb forequarter	17
Barbecued leg of lamb	18
Barbecued pork ribs	37
Barbecued steak	29
Barbecued steak sandwiches	30
Barbecued vegetable salad	80
Barbecued vegetables with polenta	71
Barbecuing techniques	6
Basics, barbecued chicken	45
Basil mayonnaise	80
Bastes and marinades	7
Beef and bean burgers	33
Beef and noodle salad, Thai-style	32
Beef fillet, festive	35
Beef patties, Sam's	34
Beef satay	55
Black bean and salmon parcels	65
Bread, garlic	84
Bread, naan	80
Brown lentil burgers	67
brown rice salad with teriyaki tuna	60
Bruschetta	84
Burgers, brown lentil	67
Butterflied lamb, tapenade rubbed	23
Cajun beef and bean burgers	33
Cakes, fresh corn	70
Caprese salad	73
Celebration salmon	63
Char-grilled Vegetable and feta salad	69
Cheesy polenta with barbecued vegetables	71
Chicken (lamb or beef) satay	55
Chicken and kumara salad	52
Chicken basics	45
Chicken legs, shortcut barbecued	46
Chicken nibbles, honey-soy	9
Chicken wings	9
Chicken, Greek barbecued	50
Chicken, red-cooked	49
Chicken, tandoori	50
Chops, lamb	19
Cleaning your barbecue	86
Coleslaw, oriental	77
Contents	3
Corn cakes, fresh	70
Corn, barbecued	79
Couscous Tabouleh	77
Cubed lamb	19
Cucumber salad	74
Curried chicken and kumara salad	52
Curried rice and pineapple salad	78
Cutlets, lamb	19
Dip, eggplant babaganoush	11
East-west marinade	17
Eggplant and feta rolls	68
Eggplant dip, babaganoush	11
Eggplant kebabs	69
Eggplant, barbecued	79
Elizabeth's favourite salad	74
Fatouish with lamb	24
Festive beef fillet	35
Festive beef marinade	35
Feta and eggplant rolls	68
Fillet, festive beef	35
Fillet, glazed pork	38
Fillet, Japanese pork	41
Fish cakes, spicy	13
Fish steaks	57
Fish tacos	59
Fish, foil wrapped	58
Flash-fried paua	13
Flounder or sole	57
Foil-wrapped fish	58
Food Safety	2
Forequarter, barbecued lamb	17
Fresh corn cakes	70
Garlic bread	84
Garlic prawns	9
Glazed pork fillet	38
Greek barbecued chicken	50
Greek salad	73
Griddle scones	84
Grilled chicken, honey-lemon	46
Grilled fish marinade	60
Grilled fish marinated	60
Ham and pasta salad	78
Ham steaks	42
Hamburgers	33
Hamburgers, Cajun beef and bean	33
Home-made hamburgers	33
Honey and yoghurt lamb	27
Honey-lemon grilled chicken	46
Honey-soy marinade	38
Honey-soy nibbles	9
Introduction	3
Japanese pork fillet	41
Jerk Lamb with kiwifruit salsa	25
Kebabs, eggplant	69
Kebabs, lamb	21
Kebabs, pork	38
Kebabs, vegetable	79
Kebabs, yoghurt and coriander chicken	53
Kebabs. Seekh lamb	20
Kiwifruit salsa	25
Korean-style barbecue chicken	49
Kumara and chicken salad	52
Kumara salad	77
Lamb and pita bread salad	24
Lamb chops and cubes	19
Lamb forequarter, barbecued	17
Lamb in yoghurt and honey	27
Lamb kebabs	21
Lamb rack	18
Lamb satay	55
Lamb souvlaki	27
Lamb, jerk	25
Leg of lamb, barbecued	18
Lemon-honey grilled chicken	46
Lentil burgers	67
Marinades	7
Marinated grilled fish	60
Marinated tomato salad	74
Mayonnaise, basil	80
Meat cooking temperatures	86
Mediterranean marinade	17
Mexican chicken	55
Mexican seasoning mix	55
Mushrooms, bacon-wrapped	10
Mushrooms, barbecued	79
Mushrooms, stuffed	67
Naan bread	83
Noisettes, lamb	19
Noodle salad, Thai-style	32
Oriental coleslaw	77
Oysters, bacon-wrapped	10
Parcels, salmon and black bean	65
Pasta and ham salad	78
Patties, Asian-style pork	42
Patties, Sam's beef	34
Paua, flash-fried	13
Peanut sauce	55
Pineapple salsa	41
Pita bread and lamb salad	24
Polenta with barbecued vegetables	71
Pork fillet, glazed	38
Pork fillet, Japanese	41
Pork fillet, stuffed	37
Pork kebabs	38
Pork patties, Asian-style	42
Pork ribs, barbecued	37
potato salad	76
potatoes barbecued	79
Prawns, garlic	9
Prunes, bacon-wrapped	10
Rack of lamb	18
Red-cooked chicken	49
Ribs, barbecued pork	37
Roasted red onion salad	80
Roasted vegetables	71
Safety	2
Salad, Asian-style beef	30
Salad, barbecued vegetable	80
Salad, brown rice with teriyaki tuna	60
Salad, char-grilled vegetable and feta	69
Salad, curried chicken and kumara	52
Salad, curried rice	78
Salad, Elizabeth's favourite	74
Salad, Greek	73
Salad, kumara	77
Salad, marinated tomato	74
Salad, pasta and ham	78
Salad, potato	76
Salad, roasted red onion	80
Salad, seared scallop and asparagus	62
Salad, Thai-style beef and noodle	32
Salad, tomato and mozzarella	73
Salad, wilted cucumber	74
Salmon and black bean parcels	65
Salmon, celebration	63
Salmon, sweet chilli on sesame noodles	65
Salsa, avocado	59
Salsa, kiwifruit	25
Salsa, pineapple	41
Sam's beef patties	34
Sandwiches, steak	30
Satay, chicken lamb or beef	55
Sauce, barbecue	37
Sauce, peanut satay	55
Sausages	15
Savouries, bacon-wrapped	10
Scallop and asparagus salad	62
Scallops, bacon-wrapped	10
Seared scallop and asparagus salad	62
Seasoning mix, Mexican	55
Seekh Kebabs	20
Sesame marinade	17
Sesame noodles with sweet chilli salmon	65
Shellfish	57
Shortcut barbecued chicken legs	46
Shoulder chops, lamb	19
Sole or flounder	57
Souvlaki, lamb	27
Soy-honey chicken nibbles	9
Spicy fish cakes	13
Steak sandwiches	30
Steak, barbecued	29
Steaks, fish	57
Stuffed mushrooms	67
Stuffed pork fillet	37
Sweet chilli salmon on sesame noodles	65
Tabouleh, couscous	77
Tacos, fish	59
Tandoori chicken	50
Tandoori marinade	50
Tapenade	23
Tapenade-rubbed butterflied lamb	23
Teriyaki-glazed tuna on Brown rice salad	60
Tex-mex marinade	17
Thai-style beef and noodle salad	32
Thai-style fish cakes	13
Tomato and mozzarella salad	73
Tomato salad	74
Tomatoes, barbecued	79
Tropical pork chops with salsa	41
Tuna, teriyaki with brown rice salad	60
Utensils	85
Vegetable kebabs, barbecued	79
Vegetables, roasted	71
Which barbecue?	4
Whole fish	57
Wilted cucumber salad	74
Wine marinade	29
Wing-a-dings	9
Yoghurt and coriander chicken kebabs	53
Yoghurt and honey lamb	27
Yoghurt marinade	53

www.hyndman.co.nz

The home of lifestyle books and gift stationery

Hyndman PUBLISHING

www.holst.co.nz

for latest news, upcoming events, recipes and sales of our books, knives and useful kitchen products